The Hidden Levels
of the Mind

The Hidden Levels of the Mind

Swedenborg's Theory of Consciousness

Douglas Taylor

With an Essay by Reuben P. Bell

Swedenborg Foundation Press

West Chester, Pennsylvania

Library of Congress Cataloging-in-Publication Data
Taylor, Douglas, 1925–
The hidden levels of the mind : Swedenborg's theory of consciousness / Douglas Taylor.
p. cm.
Includes bibliographical references.
ISBN 978-0-87785-340-4 (alk. paper)
1. Swedenborg, Emanuel, 1688-1772.   2. Consciousness.
I. Title.
BX8711.T39 2011
233'.5—dc23
2011031336

Edited by Morgan Beard
Design and typesetting by Kachergis Book Design

Printed in the United States of America

Swedenborg Foundation
320 North Church Street • West Chester, PA 19380
www.swedenborg.com

Contents

Diagrams

Preface

Beyond our everyday consciousness—the part of our mind that is constantly processing information and formulating responses, the part that we think of as "me"—there are hidden levels of our mind that exert a constant, often unfelt, influence. Sigmund Freud introduced us to the concept of a "subconscious," the part of our mind that is below our conscious awareness and houses our less-than-perfect impulses. But two centuries before Freud, a Swedish scholar named Emanuel Swedenborg (1688–1772) described what could be called the "supra-conscious," higher levels of our mind that are above our conscious awareness and can lift us up above the influence of our subconscious. We use those higher levels by living according to the Divine order as revealed in the Word of God. In this way, we slowly allow the influence of the Lord to enter us and transform our being, a process that Swedenborg calls regeneration.

Emanuel Swedenborg was born as Emanuel Svedberg in Stockholm, Sweden, on January 29, 1688, the third child and second son of Dean Jesper Svedberg and his wife, Sara Behm. At the time of Swedenborg's birth, his father was a professor of theology, and would later become a bishop in the Swedish Lutheran church. When

Jesper Svedberg was ennobled by the new queen in 1719, the family name was changed to Swedenborg.

Swedenborg's interest in science was aroused by his brother-in-law, Erik Benzelius, librarian at the University of Uppsala (Swedenborg's alma mater) and a keen student of mathematics and science. After completing his university studies in philosophy at the age of twenty, Swedenborg went on a foreign journey to complete his education. In London, he lodged with various tradespeople, learning their arts and crafts. He studied the works of Newton, introducing them to Sweden; he studied mathematics at Oxford, and conferred at length with the astronomers Flamsteed and Halley. In general, he took every opportunity to meet the world's best thinkers of his day. Looking back on this period in his old age, he recognized it as the beginning of his preparation for his life's work.

After two-and-a-half years in England, Swedenborg visited Holland, France, and Germany. At this time, his personal writings contain plans for fourteen mechanical inventions, including a submersible ship, a universal musical instrument, a flying ship, and a method of psychological analysis.

On his return to Sweden after an absence of five years, Swedenborg collaborated with Christopher Polhem, the great Swedish inventor, publishing at his own expense what is now recognized by the Swedish Academy of Sciences as its first scientific periodical. He soon received an appointment with the government ministry that oversaw the mining industry, and worked there for the next twenty-five years.

This kept him in touch with the work-a-day world, but he was also active in the learned world. He was a pioneer in geology, and he wrote the first Swedish textbook on algebra. In addition, he managed to acquire a European reputation as a first-rank philosopher. From his pen there flowed the following major works: *Philosophical* and *Mineralogical Works*; *Basic Principles of Nature* (the first volume of the three-volume work *Philosophical and Metallurgical Works*); *The Infinite*; *Dynamics of the Soul's Domain*; and *The Soul's Domain*, a sequel. As the titles of the last two books indicate, Swedenborg had become increasingly interested in the soul, specifically in a question that intrigued eighteenth-century philosophers: where is the seat or dwelling place of the soul?

In *The Soul's Domain* (published in 1744–5), Swedenborg realized that he had gone as far as reasoning from the scientific method could take him. This realization led to the turning point of his life, his transition from being a philosopher to being a theologian. He had always been a Christian philosopher, deploring the secret atheistic materialism that he encountered among a number of his scientific colleagues. His philosophic works were all designed to show that there is a realm of reality above the merely physical. He began exploring the world of spirit at age fifty-five, and he spent the next thirty years developing a remarkable theology that not only explained the way in which the soul and body interact but laid out how that interaction can bring us spiritual growth. This is the subject we will be exploring in this book.

During his lifetime, Swedenborg published eighteen theological works spread across twenty-five volumes. His teachings about the human mind are scattered throughout a number of those works, particularly *Secrets of Heaven* (often referred to by its abbreviated Latin title *Arcana Coelestia*), together with *Divine Love and Wisdom*, *Soul-Body Interaction*, and *True Christianity*. Because there is no one volume on the subject, it can be difficult to get a coherent picture of Swedenborg's philosophy of the mind. The purpose of this book is to gather together these many scattered threads and to show that, taken as a whole, they have a great relevance to our life and happiness.

This book is not intended to make you more efficient or in any other way enhance your standing in this life. The main focus will be on your *spiritual* life, your preparation for the life after death, where you may continue to grow into greater love and wisdom for eternity. Your life on this earth will not be regarded as an end in itself but a means, a means of helping you become a more spiritual kind of person, that is, an even better person.

In keeping with that purpose, this is not an exhaustive study of every passage Swedenborg ever penned on the subject of our mind. That would be a mammoth task, and one that has been very thoroughly done by the late Reverend Doctor Hugo Odhner in his book *The Human Mind*. Rather, this is a very general presentation of Swedenborg's concept of the mind, clarifying it and providing a structured framework upon which to hang his other teachings. For those interested in pursuing these ideas further, there are references throughout the book to specific passages in Swedenborg's writings. You may also be interested in one of Swedenborg's shorter works, *Divine Love and Wisdom*, which goes into greater detail about the levels of creation and the way that they relate to the human mind.

About the Source Material

The theological writings of Emanuel Swedenborg include a total of eighteen published works that originally appeared in twenty-five different volumes, and many more volumes were discovered and published posthumously. In the nearly two hundred and fifty years since Swedenborg's death, these works—the majority of which were written in Latin—have been published and republished in dozens of languages. As a consequence, even in English it is common for the same work to have been released in different times and places under different titles. For the sake of consistency, this book uses the titles as published in the New Century Edition of the Works of Emanuel Swedenborg, the most recent translation of Swedenborg's theological works.

The terms and concepts presented in this book have been translated from the Latin, and, as with the titles of Swedenborg's works, there have been many different translations over the years. The terms used in this book (for example, "will," "understanding," and "scientifics") reflect the author's preferred usage, but we have attempted to include variant translations that the reader might encounter in other books on Swedenborg's philosophy.

As is customary in Swedenborgian studies, quotations from Swedenborg's writings are referenced by section number rather than page number; the section numbers appeared in the original Latin and are uniform across all editions. Most of the quotations from Swedenborg's writings in this book have been taken from the New Century Edition. Where there were differences between the New Century Edition translations and the author's preferred terminology for Swedenborgian concepts, the author's preferred translations were used instead.

Because the New Century Edition was still a work in progress as this book was being written, we would like to thank Lisa Hyatt Cooper for providing advance translations of *Secrets of Heaven* §§1712, 1949, 1964, 2568, 3336, 3603, 5125, 5758, 5774, and 9726; and George Dole for his translation of *Soul-Body Interaction* §8 and *Life* §24.

The Hidden Levels
of the Mind

Soul, Mind, and Body

All of our conscious activity takes place in our mind. Because it is the only part of us that we can affect through our daily actions, the different levels of our mind will be the focus of this chapter, and indeed the rest of the book. However, before we can begin to describe the structure of the human mind as Emanuel Swedenborg saw it, we must first be very clear about the differences between our soul, our mind, and our body.

The Soul

Swedenborg uses the term "soul" in several different ways throughout his books, so we had better define what we mean here. In this context, our soul means the spiritual organ that receives life flowing in from the Lord. Swedenborg describes the soul as the highest or inmost part of us, the part that is nearest to the Lord—the very core of our being. The animating force of life, then, flows directly into our soul through a direct connection with the Lord.

Our soul is above our mind, so it is always beyond our conscious awareness. Even if we were to become a celestial angel—one living in the highest level of heaven—we would never be conscious of our soul (*Secrets of Heaven* §1999:3–5). You can see why this is so if you reflect for just a moment. If we were aware of what was happening in our soul, we would *feel* life flowing in. Imagine what kind of sensation that would be! It would destroy the precious feeling we all have that we are independent beings. It seems to us that we live in and of ourselves. If we were conscious of our life force flowing in from the Lord, we would lose our sense of individuality. We would no longer think of ourselves as an image and likeness of God, but as nothing more than mechanical robots. It is not simply a matter of perception: without a sense of self, a sense of individuality, there would be nothing inside us to receive and hold life from the Lord. It would flow through us unchecked. The Lord would never permit that to happen.

In *Secrets of Heaven*, Swedenborg writes:

[The Lord] cannot act on those who rid themselves of every faculty for receiving power. It is like saying that you refuse to learn anything unless it comes to you as revelation. Or like saying that you refuse to teach anything unless the words are put into your mouth. Or like refusing to try anything unless you can be propelled like an automaton. If this did happen, you would be still more resentful for feeling like an inanimate object. The reality is that what the Lord animates in us is that which seems to be ours. For instance, it is an eternal truth that life is not ours; but if it did not seem to be, we would have no life at all. (§1712:3)

Because our soul is above and beyond our conscious reach, it is impossible to pervert it. Even the evil spirits who inhabit the lowest levels of hell—who, as Swedenborg declares, were once human beings who lived in this world—have that inmost spiritual organ, the human soul. Even with these evil spirits, their human soul is always in a state of order, which is to say that it is in alignment with the Lord and receives life from him. No one's inmost soul can ever be perverted, because spiritual action always moves from higher to lower, and not the reverse. Nor is the soul ever taken away; it is always part of our being. So from a Swedenborgian perspective, no one can ever "sell their soul" or lose it through a bargain with some devil or evil spirit. The fact that we can never alter our soul in any way is one of the greatest benefits that the Lord has given us.

In our soul are two faculties that make us truly human: freedom and rationality.

The faculty of *freedom* means freedom of choice, the ability to choose between good and evil. We can see this in a definitive passage from Deuteronomy, where Moses, speaking for the Lord, says: "I call heaven and earth as witnesses today against you, that I have set before you life and death, blessing and cursing" (Deut. 30:19).

In spiritual terms, "life" means life in heaven, which is a blessing. "Death" means life in hell, which is a self-inflicted curse. That is the choice, and in Swedenborg's writings we

3

see clearly that through our motives and actions in this world, we are the ones who choose whether we will end up in heaven or in hell. But the Lord, with his infinite love, leaves no doubt about which is the better choice. He continues: "Therefore choose life, so that both you and your descendants may live." We are making this choice every day of our life.

The faculty of *rationality* means the ability to see life in the perspective of eternity, that is, to see the *ratio* between life here and life hereafter. This is clearly not the same as the worldly view of rationality, which essentially means the ability to justify whatever we wish to believe and do, whether those beliefs are true or false, good or evil. The faculty of rationality, in Swedenborg's terminology, means the ability to evaluate everything in life in a spiritual light.

Although these faculties are in our soul, we *use* them in our mind, which is where our consciousness resides. The kind of person we are is determined by the use we make of our innate faculties of freedom and rationality. That will become clearer later when we discuss in more detail the rational level of our mind. But the essential idea to remember is that the *ability* to be free and rational resides in our soul, and not in our mind.

But if our soul is different from our mind, then what is the mind?

Our Mind

A general answer might be that the mind is an organ of consciousness. This is only partly true, because there are also levels of our mind that are above our conscious awareness while we are living on earth. However, we tend to identify most often with the part of our mind that makes us aware of our surroundings in this world—the part that you are using at this very moment.

As Swedenborg states in *Divine Love and Wisdom*, at birth every human being has a soul and a body, but only the rudiments of a mind. We all know from the experience of seeing a newborn baby that he or she has very little consciousness. One of the great delights of parenthood is to watch the growth of understanding in children as they gradually become aware of the world around them.

Like our soul, our mind is made of spiritual substance. This is what distinguishes the mind from the brain. Since our brain is made entirely of physical matter, like all the organs of our body, it can be seen by our physical eyes. Not so our mind. It can never be detected by our physical senses (even when aided by a powerful microscope), because it is on a higher plane of existence. This higher plane, the mental level, is not subject to the laws of time and space. For example, in our imagination, we can we can fly, travel from one place to another in a split second, and watch our thoughts manifest themselves in front of us.

Yet our mind, though made of spiritual substance, is in one respect inferior to the soul: it does not receive love or wisdom directly from the Lord. Instead, these things enter us through the medium of the world of spirits, by thoughts and feelings flowing in from its inhabitants (*Soul-Body Interaction* §8). Just as our soul, mind, and body exist on separate levels, so does all of creation: At the highest level is heaven, where people who have lived good lives go after death; all of the angels there were once human beings living on earth, just as all of the devils in hell also were human beings. Below heaven is the world of spirits, where people of all types gather first of all after death; it is there that we discover what truly lies inside us, and whether the things that we love will pull us toward heaven or hell. All of the spirits there were once human, also, and the inhabitants of the world of spirits are closest to our physical world.

The world of spirits is the level or plane of existence that separates heaven from our physical world and acts as the medium between the two, just as our mind mediates between our soul and our body. Like our mind, the world of spirits has no physical substance and cannot be detected with any instrument; it can only be perceived by its effect on us. Swedenborg repeatedly reminds us that while our soul is above the heavens and the whole spiritual world, our mind is in the spiritual world—even now at this very moment—and is therefore subject to the influences of both good and evil spiritual forces.

We need to realize also that the mind that we use while living in this natural world "is made up of both spiritual substances and earthly substances. These latter substances fade away when we die, but the spiritual substances do not. So when we become spirits or angels after death, the same mind is still there in the form it had in the world" (Divine Love and Wisdom §257).

The same mind continues unchanged—but its function is different. In this world our "earthly mind" makes us aware of

Diagram 1. Soul, Mind, and Body

THE SOUL

The Mind

1. **Celestial**
(Love for the Lord)

2. **Spiritual**
(Love toward the Neighbor, or Charity)

3. **Natural**
(Obedience or Disobedience)

THE BODY

the world of nature. At the death of our body, however, when its natural substances recede, we can no longer be conscious of, or in, the natural world; we make the shift to become permanently conscious of and in the spiritual world. Death, then, is only a transfer of consciousness from the natural to the spiritual world, like switching the radio from one station to another. Shutting one door opens the other.

When seen in this way, our mind is also our human spirit (*Divine Love and Wisdom* §387). The same substance that we call our mind becomes the spirit when our consciousness, and thus our residence, is automatically transferred to the spiritual world after our physical body dies.

Swedenborg describes the mind as being organized on three distinct levels or grades of mental activity: the natural or earthly, the spiritual, and the celestial or heavenly (*Divine Love and Wisdom* §237). In the original Latin, he used the term *gra-*

dus, meaning a step or grade, to describe these levels. In the past, this term has usually been translated as "a degree." However, with some readers of Swedenborg that has been confusing, and the concept has acquired an aura of mystery, particularly when the term *discrete degrees* is used. The term *degree* refers simply to different levels of mental activity; when the word *discrete* is attached, it means that these levels exist separately and cannot be thought of as mixing together. It is important to attach clear ideas to those terms; otherwise they will become almost meaningless words that are easily repeated mindlessly. Accordingly, we will use the word *level* instead of *degree.*

Swedenborg describes the three levels of our mind in this way:

The mind of man, which consists of will and understanding, is from creation, and therefore from birth, of three levels, so that man has a natural mind, a spiritual mind, and a celestial mind, and can thereby be elevated into and possess angelic wisdom while he lives in the world; but it is only after death, and then only if he becomes an angel, that he enters into that wisdom, and his speech then becomes ineffable and incomprehensible to the natural man. (*Divine Love and Wisdom* §239)

That passage says that we can be "elevated into and possess angelic wisdom" while living in this world, but that is referring only to our potential. It is nothing more than a possibility. We all have that wisdom implicitly, but we enter into it according to our life on earth and use it fully and explicitly only after death and if we become an angel.

The highest level of our mind, the celestial, receives love

from the Lord—the purest form of love, and the part of our self that manifests it most clearly. It is the fulfillment of the first and greatest commandment: "You shall love the Lord your God with all your heart, with all your soul, and with all your mind" (Matt. 22:37). With regard to conscious understanding, this part of our mind receives the divine wisdom—the ability to see all things in heavenly light—that is the offspring of divine love.

The spiritual mind or level of mental activity consists of love of others and feelings of goodwill or charity. In the next verse of Matthew, the Lord identifies this as the second of the two great commandments: "You shall love your neighbor as yourself" (Matt. 22:39). When we experience this love and express it in words or actions, we are saying what we *really* believe.

We gain a fuller understanding of these two commandments when we realize that in the Greek of the New Testament there are two words for love: one means "to be fond of" and the other means "to consider the welfare of." The second word is used in both commandments, and elsewhere whenever we are *commanded* to love. The Lord can certainly command us to consider the welfare of others: that is real love, an outgoing love. But no one, not even the Lord, can command us "to be fond" of another. That happens spontaneously or it does not happen at all. We are either fond of a person or we are not fond. It is a personal matter. Consequently, the Lord is not commanding us to be fond of everyone; but he is commanding us to consider the welfare of others—whether we like them or not. Verses that mention our love for the Lord have a similar meaning. Our salvation does not depend on our being "fond" of the Lord, but on considering his welfare and that of his kingdom. That is why he said: "He who has my commandments and keeps them, it is he who loves me" (John 14:21).

The two higher levels of the mind, the celestial and the spiritual, constitute what Swedenborg calls the *internal* mind (see diagram 2). We can also think of it as the supra-conscious mind, as opposed to the conscious mind and the subconscious mind that Sigmund Freud wrote about. While the subconscious mind exists below our conscious awareness and houses our less-than-perfect impulses, the supra-conscious mind exists above our conscious awareness and can lift us up above the influences of the subconscious. This internal mind is in contrast to the external or natural mind, which we will discuss below.

Spiritually speaking, the internal mind obviously belongs to heaven, since its ruling or predominant love is either love for the Lord or charity toward the neighbor. In fact, it could also be called the heavenly mind. This is where the Lord dwells with us.

It is important to realize that everyone, no matter what his or her heredity or environment, has that internal mind. There are no exceptions. As we read in Swedenborg's *Secrets of Heaven*, "In the internal mind are nothing else than goods and truths that are the Lord's . . . In every person [there is] a celestial and a spiritual level that corresponds to the angelic heaven" (§978; see also §1594:5).

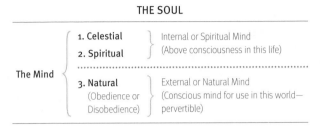

Diagram 2. The Structure of Our Mind

THE SOUL

	1. Celestial	Internal or Spiritual Mind
	2. Spiritual	(Above consciousness in this life)
The Mind	3. Natural	External or Natural Mind
	(Obedience or	(Conscious mind for use in this world—
	Disobedience)	pervertible)

THE BODY

Although our internal mind is above our conscious aware-ness while we are on earth, when we pass into the spiritual world (and if we become an angel there), we gain the wisdom of either the spiritual or the celestial level of heaven, depend-ing on which one of those two higher levels of our mind most often flowed down into us while we were living in this world.

In marked contrast to the sublime reaches of our internal mind is the conscious mind that we use in our daily life: the lowest level of our mind, the natural or earthly level. If you are reading this book and understanding it (or even not under-standing it!) you are using your conscious mind, which is also called the external mind. This, Swedenborg often points out, is not the same thing as our brain. Since the mind is the per-son, the term external mind refers to that part of us that is con-scious of the world around us. Our body (of which the brain is a part) exists only to allow us to function on the physical plane.

So wherever you find the terms "external mind" or "natural mind" in this book, keep this distinction in mind.

With the internal mind focused on heaven and the external mind focused on this world, it's easy to see how the two can be in conflict. This is the cause of our temptations; they represent our struggle to make our external mind submit to our higher levels. Our natural mind is the only part of us that can be out of heaven's order, cause trouble, and be perverted. It often is— we all know that from experience! It is our natural mind that *exercises* free will, and it is there that we choose either to obey the Lord or disobey. When our external mind is aligned with our internal mind, it is because we have chosen self-compelled obedience.

Our natural or external mind, then, is the source of all our problems, individually and collectively. In order for us to progress spiritually and move toward heaven, our natural mind needs to be reformed and regenerated—to be reborn. This, says Swedenborg, is what is meant by John 3:3: "Most assuredly, I say to you, unless one is born again, he cannot see the kingdom of God."

In order for this to happen, our internal mind must take possession of and transform our external mind. But how is this done? How, in other words, can we let heaven's influence flow into us?

A short answer would be: We have to shun our evils *because they are sins against the Lord* and not for any lesser or worldly reason, such as self-aggrandizement or social status.

A more comprehensive answer is that while we are born

with a natural mind, it is only the beginning. We can develop our understanding by means of what we learn from the world around us. We could go on learning and learning and learning for the rest of our life; we could gain two or three university degrees; we could even acquire an impressive understanding of the Bible, the Word of God. But we would still remain natural in quality unless we began to live according to that understanding.

The more we live according to the Word, the more we are motivated by real goodness. Our actions begin to become spiritual in quality, because the spiritual level of our internal mind is opened. If this happens, our natural mind will be opened at the top, so that what exists at the spiritual level of the mind (charity or love toward the neighbor) could flow down into our conscious mind and move us in our everyday lives.

However, above the spiritual level of our mind is the celestial level. If we were to go on living a life of charity for the rest of our lives, we would indeed become heavenly, but we would never rise above that middle spiritual level. To go beyond that, we need to come into celestial love—loving the Lord (or rather, having his love come into us). We accomplish that by obeying the Lord's commandments for his sake rather than any selfish thought of promoting ourselves. In that way, love and concern for the Lord flow down into our natural mind, making it celestial or spiritual in quality (see *Divine Love and Wisdom* §237).

Because we have free will, we can also choose to keep our natural mind closed at the top, so that none of these higher loves can flow in. That happens to the extent that we do not live according to what the Word of God teaches us to believe and do. In that case, we would remain the same forever, even in the spiritual world, and never be able to experience heaven's love.

In summary, regeneration or rebirth consists in allowing the higher levels of our mind to act upon our natural level, transforming it and making it spiritual or celestial in quality. (There is a fuller explanation of regeneration in chapter 2.) However, these levels do not simply merge one into the other; they remain distinctly separate, which is the idea behind the concept of "discrete degrees" discussed above. These levels also remain distinct from the brain and the body where it lives.

The Body

The body is not the person. The mind is the person. By and large, the world around us is profoundly ignorant of that fact. What is the usual reply when you ask people, "How are you today?" You are often treated to a recital of their aches and pains or their current disease. That is perfectly understandable, because people do tend to think of the body as the person. Shape and appearance are often among what first come to mind when a person is named. That is especially the case with little children. They experience what is probably their first great shock when they realize that a beautiful-looking person does not necessarily have a character to match. Young people also, when they are searching for their future married partner, tend to think that physical appearance is the most valuable attribute. Subconsciously, they are equating the body with the person. But doctrine, experience, and common sense unite to tell us that this is not necessarily so. We all know on reflection that we are to judge people by the quality of their minds.

Swedenborg writes that the doctrine of resurrection of the physical body following the Last Judgment was actually the result of confusing the body with the person. In truth, he tells us, human beings are resurrected in the spirit—in the world of spirits, which, as discussed in the previous chapter, is where we awaken after our physical bodies cease to function. Only the Lord was resurrected in his physical body.

The body includes the brain, so the brain is not the person either, despite the fact that we speak of "brainy" people, as if their intellectual superiority was entirely due to their brains alone, as if the brain (made of physical matter) and the mind (made of spiritual substance) were identical.

That overemphasis on the physical seems to prevail in materialistic philosophies such as logical positivism, whose adherents propound the theory that the mind is not a thing at all. It is simply a word, they say, a word used to describe the functioning of the brain. The mind is therefore said to be a mere abstraction, while the brain is favored as something tangible and perceptible. Those who think in this way are what Swedenborg calls sensuous people, because they believe only what they can see with their eyes and feel with their hands (Secrets of Heaven §§5094, 7693).

Swedenborg describes the brain as the organ or link by which the mind acts into the body as a whole; it is the entrance-point of the mind into the body. Divine love and wisdom, he says, descend from heaven through the internal mind, into the

Diagram 3. Highest and Inmost

What is closest to God is at the highest level . . .

. . . but when viewed from above it becomes the inmost.

external mind, and from there into the cerebellum (where our affections live) and finally into our cerebrum, where our understanding is (*Revelation Explained* §61). Thus, he sums up the relationship between mind, body, and soul in this way: "Since the human soul is a higher, spiritual substance, it receives an inflow directly from God. The human mind, though, being a lower spiritual substance, receives an inflow from God indirectly through the spiritual world; while the body, being made of the earthly substances we refer to as matter, receives an inflow from God indirectly through the earthly world" (*Soul-Body Interaction* §8).

Throughout this book, the parts of our self that are closest to the Lord will sometimes be referred to as the highest, and sometimes as the inmost. In Swedenborg's writings, the two are one and the same. Diagram 3 illustrates this concept more clearly: While the levels of our being have a definite order, with the most heavenly level being the highest, when viewed from above, the highest becomes the inmost.

Because all of our conscious thought and feelings—every idea and desire that makes up the personality that we think of as our self—take place in the natural mind, that will be the focus of the remainder of the book. The natural mind itself has many levels, and we will give an overview of those in the next chapter.

The Levels of Our Natural Mind

We have been discussing the three major levels of our mind as a whole—the natural, the spiritual, and the celestial—as being three separate, ascending levels, also called *discrete degrees*. Each level is of a different quality from the others: the predominant love or motivation that rules the natural level is either obedience or disobedience to the commandments of the Lord; that of the spiritual level is loving the good in one's neighbor, also called charity; that of the celestial is loving the Lord above all else.

We are now going to learn that in our natural mind there are also levels, but they are of an entirely different kind. They are not separate levels distinguished by the quality of the love that motivates them, for our entire natural mind (if left to itself without any higher influences) is of one and the same unchanging quality—natural! Instead, the levels of our natural mind are distinguished from each other by the different functions that each one performs, regardless of the motive from which they are done. These functions are:

1. *Sensation.* Using our five senses opens this lowest level of the natural mind—the first to develop in infants. This part of the mind is called the *sensory level.*

2. *Generalization.* Based on the information from our senses, we draw conclusions about what people and natural things do. These conclusions open and form what is called the *middle natural level* of our mind.

3. *Sense of Proportion.* The ability to distinguish between what is natural and what is spiritual. This function belongs to the highest level of our natural mind, called the *rational level* because it enables us to see the *ratio* between the spiritual and the natural.

These functional levels develop one after the other, beginning with the sensory level, and mark the three main stages in the mental growth of our natural mind. These stages are sometimes described as if they were discrete levels, and there is indeed a distinct progression from one level to the other. However, taken in the broader context of our human mind, these levels are all part of our external mind. Their functions are all of a natural or earthly quality—the type of thought that takes place before regeneration. Although the external mind is only a small part of who we are, it is the part that we most identify as our "self" because it is where our everyday consciousness dwells. These three functional levels of our external mind will therefore be the focus of the remaining chapters of this book, because it

Diagram 4. Functional Levels of
Our Natural Mind

Sense of Proportion The Rational Level

Generalization The Middle Natural Level

Sensation The Sensory Level

---

is here that regeneration begins—if it is going to begin at all. In this chapter we will give only a brief overview of the three levels, leaving a fuller treatment of them for later chapters.

The Sensory Level

As we all know, the first kind of mental activity in which children engage is sensation. Babies love to experience the things around them with all five senses—especially touch and taste. It is remarkable what dangerous things they want to put into their mouths! They are using the sensory level of their mind, and at first, that is the only type of mental activity we can observe in newborn infants. But even at this very early stage, sensory impressions of the people and objects of the world around them are being stored up in their minds.

Swedenborg teaches that the Lord's special angels from the highest heaven, whose gentle influence surrounds babies at this time, instill celestial delights into their opening mind: "In heaven their angels always see the face of my Father who is in heaven" (Matt. 18:10). These heavenly delights are unconsciously associated in the baby's mind with the impressions they receive through their senses. Swedenborg calls these delights and images the "remains of good and truth," and they become the foundation for the growing child's loves and desires. Every newborn is gifted with these "remains," regardless of their heredity or environment, but sadly in some cases such remains may be the only remnants of heavenly delights that they ever experience or can draw upon in later life. Parents clearly have a great responsibility in regard to the spiritual life of their children as well as to their natural life.

There is also the intellect or understanding, even at this stage. To call it the intellect seems like a misnomer, because it consists only of sensory images of things seen, heard, touched, tasted, or smelled. These images remain in the natural memory and are called forth to help form the imagination at a later stage in the development of this sensory level of our mind.

The Middle Natural Level

As they grow, children are able to engage in a more refined form of mental activity. They now begin to focus, not merely on the forms of things, but on what those things do or how they behave. This is an advance on mere sensation. The child is now making generalizations or forming conclusions or laws about those images that have come into their minds by way of the sensory level. Swedenborg's term for those generalizations is *scientifics*. Although the children aren't yet aware of it, by drawing conclusions based on their sense perceptions they are being little scientists, using the scientific method (*Secrets of*

Heaven §5774:2). They *conclude* scientifics. This opens the middle level of their natural mind, called the middle natural. This provides a basis for the rational level—the highest level of mental activity in our natural mind.

The two lower levels of our natural mind—the sensory and the middle natural—can be opened simply by experience, by receiving sense impressions and by drawing conclusions from them. Even an atheist can have those two levels opened. But something more is needed to open the rational level, the highest level of our natural mind.

The Rational Level

The function of the mind's rational level, as Swedenborg defines it, is to be the bridge between what is natural and what is spiritual. For that reason, in order to open the rational level of our mind, we need to have at least some knowledge of the Word of God, which tells us about the spiritual world and things spiritual. Without such instruction, we would never know anything beyond this natural world and its laws. We would be completely in the dark about the supra-natural level of our mind, which is above the world of nature. We would have no concept of the relationship between life in the natural world and life in the spiritual world, because for us in our ignorance the spiritual world and spiritual things would be seem to be nonexistent. In that case, we would not be able to live according to spiritual laws; we cannot live what we do not know.

The rational level of our mind develops in adolescence; it is the point at which we must at least try to start living in accordance with spiritual laws. However, the rational level does not open to the higher levels of our mind, the internal mind, unless we choose to begin the process of regeneration by co-operating with the Lord.

Regeneration

When we turn to the Lord, we begin to experience a rebirth of the spirit, something that Swedenborg calls regeneration. This is a process, not an event occurring in one glorious day—a gradual change in our thoughts and affections that lifts our minds from its everyday natural state to a more spiritual one.

Living according to what we have learned from the Word not only opens the rational level but also regenerates it, changing its quality from natural to spiritual. That is accomplished gradually to the extent that what is above in our internal mind—that is, charity or love of the neighbor (the spiritual level) and love for the Lord (the celestial)—begin to flow down into the rational level, altering its quality completely. The rational level of the mind is gradually "born from above" (John 3:3) and is no longer of a natural quality, but is either spiritual or celestial, depending on which of these qualities is flowing in from our internal mind.

A similar process takes place with our middle natural level. It is "born again" or "born from above" as the heavenly qualities of the *regenerated* rational level flow down into it. The middle natural level is then regenerated and also becomes either spiritual or celestial in quality.

Then finally, our sensory level becomes subject to the born-

Diagram 5. Ascent and Descent in Regeneration

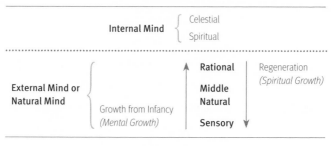

THE SOUL

		Celestial
	Internal Mind ⎰	
		Spiritual

		⬆	Rational	Regeneration
				(Spiritual Growth)
External Mind or	⎱		Middle	
Natural Mind			Natural	
	Growth from Infancy			
	(Mental Growth)		Sensory ⬇	

THE BODY

again levels above it. The person is then fully regenerated; even his sensory level, the lowest level of his or her mind, has been put in alignment with heaven as far as possible (*Secrets of Heaven* §7442:4).

Notice in diagram 5 that in the growth of our mind from the time we are infants there is an ascent from the lowest level to the highest; but in its regeneration, there is a descent from the highest down to the lowest. That may remind you of the story of Jacob's ladder in the book of Genesis: "Then he dreamed, and behold, a ladder was set up on the earth, and its top reached to heaven; and there the angels of God were ascending and descending on it" (Gen. 28:12).

There was an ascent and then a descent. In the literal story that is a puzzle; we ask ourselves, why is it said that the angels ascended and then descended? People usually think of the angels as being "up there," so they would surely have descended and then ascended. But when we learn from Swedenborg's interpretation of the spiritual meaning within the Word of God that the reference is first to the growth of our mind (an ascent), and afterward to its regeneration (a descent from the highest down to the lowest), then that whole vision of Jacob's ladder is filled with a new meaning and relevance that it did not have for us before.

The Will and the Understanding

Every level of our external mind has two parts: the will and the understanding (sometimes translated volition and discernment).

The will can be thought of as the home of our affections and emotions, but it also includes all of the impulses that drive us. The will is the part of our mind that desires things, or that urges us to do this thing or that thing because it feels good. Often we are unaware or only partly aware of what our will is pushing us to do; this is what we mean when we talk about unconscious impulses. Note that the will is not limited to the purely physical instincts that come from the body. Those instincts are automatic responses over which we have no control, whereas the will relates to our deliberate responses to our desires.

Swedenborg writes about each person's ruling or dominant love, by which he means the thing that a person loves more than anything else. He breaks ruling loves into four categories. The first two are love of the Lord and love of the neighbor, which are the two good kinds of ruling love. The two evil ones are love of the world and love of self. Love of the world here does not mean having positive feelings toward the *people* of the world, but rather an inordinate desire for material pleasures. For example, people who will do anything to be famous, even if it means hurting family or friends, are ruled by their love of prestige, which is a form of love of the world.

While living on earth, we may have loves or affections for many different things, but after we pass over into the spiritual world, it will gradually become clear which one predominates. That ruling love develops in the will of our external mind as we live and grow here on earth.

It is important to note that the term *affection* has a very specific meaning in Swedenborg's writings and among students of his work. Affection is not limited to liking a person or thing; it also means the way that we react to things like spiritual truth or good. This is illustrated in *Secrets of Heaven* §3876: "When a person is affected by truth, that is, when he perceives delight and blessedness in acting according to truth, he is then in charity."

Our understanding or intellect is, as the name implies, the part of our mind that processes information and develops new ideas. Whereas the will can be largely subconscious, the understanding is our conscious mind at work. It is the part of our mind that not only thinks but imagines outcomes, for good or evil.

One might be tempted to blame our will for leading us astray—as it often does!—but coming to false conclusions about the world around us, particularly about spiritual matters, can be just as dangerous. Both the will and the understanding must be regenerated, on all levels of our mind, before we can truly experience the light of heaven.

Our Sensory Level

The sensory level is the lowest kind of mental activity there is, because this is the level where we all begin as infants. We experience the objects, animals, and people of the natural, physical world while they are before our senses. Infants may also recall what they've experienced when those things are not present, summoning the images of them that they have in their natural memory; they may also use those images to imagine future outcomes.

Writing in Latin, Swedenborg used the word *sensualis*, which is often translated as "sensual" or "sensuous." However, the term *sensory* is preferable to *sensual*, because the latter word has undergone a certain degradation since Swedenborg's day. In today's language, a sensual person means what Swedenborg calls a *corporeal* or bodily person, one who is a slave to his or her appetites. The term *sensory*, by contrast, refers to what comes into our mind by way of any of the five senses. It does not refer exclusively to the appetites, nor does it necessarily have a pejorative sense, and is therefore a more accurate translation of *sensualis*.

On the sensory level of our mind, the will is made up of the pleasures of the senses—seeing beautiful things, hearing wonderful sounds, and so on. The understanding, on the other hand, is simply sensing objects, even when there is not yet any comprehension. At this stage, the understanding is forming mental images of material objects and things outside of us. Swedenborg calls these mental images *material ideas*, a term that is sometimes translated "matter-based ideas" (*Secrets of Heaven* §10604:1, 2).

As we discussed in the chapter on soul, body, and mind, when discussing the sensory level of the mind it is important to draw a distinction between the physical senses—which are of the body—and our mind, which is composed of a spiritual substance. Swedenborg tells us that the physical eye does not see. "It is according to an appearance that the eye sees; but it is the intellect that sees by means of the eye; consequently seeing is said also of the intellect" (*Divine Love and Wisdom* §363). The eye receives light waves and transmits them via the nervous system to the brain, which is thereby changed according to the form of those light waves. But it is our mind that senses and interprets those changes according to its knowledge, understanding, and interests.

A geologist, an artist, and a farmer might look at the same rocky mountain, but their eyes would see three different mountains. The geologist would be thrilled with the examples of the Mesozoic rocks and the (obvious for him) history of their formation; the artist would be very moved by the colors and the grandeur of the magnificent silhouette; the farmer might grumble, "You couldn't grow any crops up there!"

Two actual cases from a psychology textbook give further confirmation of the subjectivity of many of our sensory observations. In the first one, a group of students was asked to go without food for three days. At the end of that time, they were presented with a Rorschach test, a sheet of paper on which were ink blots that could be interpreted in various ways by the mind of the viewer. When asked to write down what they saw, many reported seeing steaks, hot dogs, hamburgers, and other foods in the amorphous shapes!

In the second case, a young man was eagerly awaiting the death of his rich old uncle, from whom he expected to receive a sizable inheritance. In his imagination he had already pictured how he would spend it. But at the reading of the will, he was shattered to find that he was to receive nothing at all. He was in shock and denial, with the result that he immediately became psychosomatically blind. He was unable to bear the sight of that miserable will.

We can see from the above examples that while our body collects sensory input, it is our mind that does the interpretation. The part of our mind that does the interpretation is what Swedenborg calls the external sensory. It is the lowest or outermost part of our sensory level, and therefore the lowest part of our mind. Perhaps the most concise definition is given in this passage in *Secrets of Heaven*: "The external sensory is not the sense of the body itself, such as sight, smelling, hearing, touch, taste, but what is most nearly from these" (§9730).

What would be "most nearly from these"? It would be the mental images of things sensed, what we saw earlier as material ideas. These images or ideas become the basis of our thoughts and affections, first formed in our infancy. Infants learn to think by sensing the world around them, and they quickly learn to identify the things that are pleasing to their senses (*Revelation Explained* §543:2).

But then, if the eyes with which we see the natural world are really the eyes of our spirit, why is it that while living in this world, we do not see the objects of the spiritual world or see what is happening there?

In answering that question, we must begin by pointing out that in both the natural world and the spiritual world, seeing requires three things:

1. An object to be seen
2. An organ of sight
3. Light by which the object can be seen

The crucial difference lies in the third point. Just as there is light in the natural world, there is also light in the spiritual world, but spiritual light has a completely different essence. Swedenborg describes spiritual light as being derived from a spiritual sun that is pure love, or life itself; whereas natural light comes from the sun we see in the sky, which is made of physical elements and has no life in and of itself. Angels in heaven have eyes that were designed to see that spiritual light in the same way that we see physical light; but because the two lights are very different in nature, the eyes that can see one type of light cannot perceive the other (*Divine Love and Wisdom* §§90, 91).

From that explanation we may understand why we are not able to see the things in the spiritual world, although our minds—being made of spiritual substance—are there. Our minds are the bridge between the physical and spiritual worlds, and they are also the filter that determines what we see and understand. Because the physical stimuli from the world around us are so strong, they tend focus our attention on the physical substances of the natural world while we are living here. However, we can also choose to become more aware of the spiritual world's impact on us.

It is a very merciful truth that we are not obliged to experience every light-wave and every sound-wave that strikes our sense receptors. Just imagine how overwrought we would become if we had to experience fully everything that impinged upon our five senses—every sound, every sight, every touch, and every odor. That would be, to say the least, cruel and unusual punishment!

For that reason we are very selective in what we attend to, and that is why our external sensory is symbolized in the Word of God by a grate. "The senses," we read, "function as an initial screen or filter for incoming impressions that are passed on to the intellect and the will, and consequently for truth and goodness. If the sensory plane is sound, it lets in only good affections, and true ideas that spring from something good. It rejects evil, and falsity that springs from evil. This is because the senses are exactly the means by which the intellect and will gather perceptions and sensations on the outermost level. They are formed precisely to respond to such stimuli" (*Secrets of Heaven* §9726).

The things that our external sensory allows to enter our minds are stored in our natural or exterior memory (as opposed to our interior memory, which contains principles that come from our spiritual values).

For the most part we have so far been considering the exterior of the sensory level, the outer form of sensation—using our physical senses. But there is also an inner aspect to the sensory level, and it is what we know as the imagination. Swedenborg describes it this way: "To the natural mind also belongs all the imaginative faculty, which is an interior sensory with man and which is in the greatest vigor with children and in the first age of adolescence" (*Secrets of Heaven* §3020:2).

Sometimes the description of the imagination differs very little from that of the memory. They are both a collection of mental images. We can take out from our memory images of things in the past, concentrate on them, and relive them. But we have to be careful to separate memory from imagination. They are not the same, as witness Mark Twain's comment about his aunt: "She could remember everything, whether it happened or not!"

After all, what do we do when we imagine something? We picture that object in "our mind's eye." The English poet Wordsworth, in a poem about his beloved daffodils, said that when he thought about them, "they flash upon that inward eye, which is the bliss of solitude." All he had to do was to recall the images of them from his memory; but we cannot do that, because we have not actually seen the daffodils. As we read his poetic description of them, we have to imagine them. We have to use our interior sensory level.

When we think of imagination, we think of looking forward—modifying and changing the images that are in the memory, reshaping them, putting them into new relationships and combinations. That is what inventors do, making it possible to create new things and to improve on old ones. This type of forward-looking visualization is what we usually mean when we commend a person for being imaginative.

We have seen that the exterior of the sensory level is like a kind of grate that selects what we wish to concentrate upon. The same is true of our interior sensory, the imagination. What causes us to choose certain images out of our memory and reject others? What leads us to modify them into new forms in our imagination?

It is always an affection—the feeling attached to memories and experiences—that rouses up the images of our memory and forms our imagination. Affection is the heart and soul of imagination, and indeed of all levels of mental activity.

As we read in *Secrets of Heaven*:

It is possible to recognize that absolutely nothing can enter our memory and stay there unless some affection, some form of love, introduces it. If there were no affection—that is, no love—there would not be any awareness. That affection, or that love, is what connects with the information as it enters and, once connected, keeps it there. This stands to reason if you consider that when a similar affection or love returns, the information reappears, bringing with it many other pieces of information memorized earlier at the call of a similar affection or love, and so on in a chain. That is the source of our thoughts and, from our thought, of our speech. By the same token, when we remember the information, whether prompted by objects of the senses, or objects of thought, or another's words, the affection that introduced it into our memory also returns. (§3336:2)

We have been looking mainly at the thinking side of the sensory level of our mind, what Swedenborg calls the understanding, and have learned that it consists of material ideas. But the quality of our sensory level—or of any level of our mind—can be known only from the will, which is our feeling side. What we love determines what kind of person we are. The will is the person himself or herself.

On our sensory level, the will consists of the pleasures of the senses, delights associated with things sensed or imagined. This is especially the case with the senses of touch and taste. In themselves these pleasures are neutral, neither good nor evil. They become good or evil depending on the use to which they are put. If these pleasurable sensations are used for the sake of refreshing or relaxing our mind so that we may return to our duties with renewed energy, then they are good and useful. But if these pleasures are indulged in for their own sake entirely, they are no longer good or neutral but evil, abused for self-gratification. As adults, before we are regenerated, we tend to be self-indulgent. Therefore, we can say that the dominant love that rules people at the sensory level is the love of self. This is where it lives. If our will for the most part never rises higher than the sensory level, we are *sensuous* or *corporeal* people (*Secrets of Heaven* §5094:2).

Of course, with babies and infants the situation is different, for every one of them is under angelic influences and protection. They inherit from their parents and ancestors tendencies to be delighted by evil (though not actual evils themselves; Swedenborg rejects the idea of original sin). However, with babies those tendencies are always kept quiescent and under subjection to the tender sphere of the highest angels, thus providing the necessary counterbalance to give growing minds freedom of choice. There are no exceptions. That is why every newborn begins life under the auspices of the Lord and his angels, regardless of its heredity or environment. That is the source of the universally recognized sphere of innocence that radiates from the newly born.

Swedenborg describes sensuous people as being focused solely on the world around them, believing in nothing except for what they can see and touch, their minds being closed to inner truth. Because they cannot experience heavenly things directly, they reject the idea of heaven, relying solely on their *external* memory for information. Sensuous people are sometimes so focused on their own self-gratification that they become malicious, hurting other people and committing the sins of greed or adultery. Others, however, simply have not learned to cultivate the rational level of their minds, which is the part where we evaluate our lives in the perspective of eternity.

Cultivating the rational level of our mind—whether done as a growing young person or as an adult seeking greater meaning—is a crucial step in regeneration. However, the rational level is not formed immediately; first, we have to develop what Swedenborg calls the *middle natural level* as a basis for the rational level. That will be our topic in the next chapter.

Our Middle Natural Level

The kind of mental activity that takes place on the middle of the natural level is above sensation. It is not a matter of receiving sensory impressions of particular objects or people as they are, strictly according to their appearance; at this level we are forming conclusions or laws about what all such objects or people do and how they behave. It could therefore be called the level of generalization.

With regard to our intellect, the conclusions, laws, or generalizations that make up the middle natural level are drawn from our sense observations. In the past some translations of Swedenborg's theological writings have used the term *memory knowledges* for those doctrinal teachings that have been committed to memory, but not to life—in other words, the things we know but do not put into practice. But that term is not very satisfactory. After all, every piece of knowledge we have must be in our memory; otherwise it is nowhere. Therefore, it is much better to refer to these doctrinal teachings as *scientifics*, or things known, because that is what they are—that is, they are *merely* known, without being incorporated into our daily lives.

For example, let us consider a fire. We can see, hear, feel, or smell a fire. But if we limit our experience to that sensory level, we really cannot say that we *know* a fire. Once we describe what we know about a fire—how it works and what it does—we have moved up to the middle natural level. We have gone beyond mere sensory-level gazing.

Whatever describes how something in this world works or what it does is a scientific or a law of science, a description of how a thing works. As discussed in the chapter on soul, mind, and body, we *conclude* scientifics by observing with our senses how things work or people behave, or else we are taught the conclusions that others have formed from their observations. Even little children advance beyond mere sensation and begin to generalize from their sense experience. For example, if they say, "Fire burns you," they have formed a conclusion or scientific based on their experience—sometimes a rather painful experience.

The difference between the sensory level and the middle natural level is clearly brought out in *Secrets of Heaven* §5774:2:

Sensory information is one thing, generalizations [scientifics] are another, and truth is another. They follow one after the other, because generalizations develop out of sense impressions, and truth develops out of generalizations. Impressions entering through our senses are stored in our memory, and we draw generalizations as conclusions from them, or else we perceive in them the facts we are learning. From generalizations we draw truth as a conclusion, or we perceive in them the truth we are learning. That is how we move forward from youth as we grow up. When we are young, we use sense impressions as a basis for thought and comprehension. When we grow older we use generalizations as a basis for thought and comprehension, and still later we use truth. This is the path to acquiring the power of judgment, which we grow into as we mature.

But we need to know that with Swedenborg, scientifics are not limited to laws or conclusions about the way things work in the natural world. That is the usual way the term *science* is used today: it is restricted for the most part to physical things that obey the laws of physics. But in Swedenborg's day the term science included also our conclusions regarding the behavior of people—how people *choose* to behave, in contrast to the way things inevitably work. This is obviously a deeper kind of generalizing than forming laws about merely physical things. The concept of human freedom to choose has entered the scene. This level, because it is about people, is on a deeper level than physical objects and therefore could be called the inner middle natural level, while the first kind of generalizing, being limited to the physical level, is called the outer middle natural level.

We will look first at the scientifics of the exterior middle natural level. They are in general the familiar disciplines that used to be studied under the old name of natural philosophy. Nowadays we all know them as science (pure and applied). The laws or branches of study include, but are not limited to: physics, chemistry, medicine, engineering, various manual skills, trades, crafts, and techniques; also some aspects of economics and architecture—all related to the way things in the physical world work, and the effects they produce. All those conclusions or things known are acquired by the scientific method. The focus now is not on the objects themselves, but on the way they work and what they do. Those examples help explain why Swedenborg says that the exterior of the middle natural level communicates with the outside world, and vice versa (*Secrets of Heaven* §10236).

The contents of the interior of the middle natural level, on the other hand, include conclusions from sensory experience about human beings and how they behave. This would include all the fields of study usually called the humanities, such as languages, literature, sociology, anthropology, history, the nonreligious aspects of philosophy, the nonphysical aspects of psychology and psychiatry, art in general, music, and any studies of manners and customs of peoples, or the techniques of human relations. In fact, any discipline involving human conduct is to be included in the interior natural level. An interesting case is the subject of geography. It belongs partly to the exterior and partly to the interior of the middle natural level, because the physical aspects of geography that are very similar to geology relate to the exterior, whereas the more human aspects of geography, the customs of peoples in various lands, their languages, and so on, would properly belong in the interior of the middle natural level.

By far the most important example of the interior middle natural level—at least, as far as the intellect is concerned—is knowledge of the moral virtues. The knowledge of these virtues is what communicates above all else with the next highest level of the natural mind, the rational level, as we will soon see. In his work *Marriage Love*, Swedenborg provides a list of the moral virtues: temperance, sobriety, probity, benevolence, friendship, modesty, sincerity, civility, assiduity, industry, alertness, alacrity, munificence, liberality, generosity, earnestness, intrepidity, and prudence (§164).

It is important to understand that all scientifics, including all the moral virtues, look no further than to life in this natural world. That is why this level is called the middle *natural*. There is no looking to spiritual ends, no consideration of anything higher than this life. It is simply limited to actions, not motives. Such is the quality of the understanding of anyone whose mind has not developed to anything higher than the middle natural level.

However, our middle natural level as a whole is closer to the internal mind than the sensory level is. It is further removed or abstracted from the mere objects of time and space that are experienced by the senses. The sensory level consists of *nothing but* ideas related to time and space—material ideas—even at the interior of the sensory level, the imagination. But the imagination is a little less confined to physical objects than is the exterior sensory level, because in the imagination we can defy the laws of time and space. So it is one step removed from the fixation upon visual imagery that confines us to the exterior sensory level.

Overall, we can say that the middle natural level is made up of generalizations or conclusions that are abstract ideas. They are based on our sensory impressions, but they are concerned with the way that objects and people behave anywhere, any time.

With very little children, the interior natural level is only beginning to be opened. While they can understand the difference between the behavior of a good man and a bad man, they do not as yet really understand an abstract concept like good and evil. As Swedenborg puts it: "From childhood to early youth, communication is opened with the interior natural level by learning what is becoming, what the civil laws require, and what is honorable both by instruction from parents and teachers and by studies" (*Secrets of Heaven* §5126:3).

The need to attend to moral virtues and decorum cannot be overemphasized. If that plane, or level, of our mind is not formed by instruction and example, and opened by living a life according to those moral virtues, there can be no communication with the rational level and, through that, with the internal mind.

But what of the will side of the middle natural level? What loves or affections would constitute it?

The middle natural level (before regeneration) is moved by a love of the world, in particular by the delights associated with learning. In some cases this may be an inborn love of learning, or a desire to make discoveries about things and people in this physical world. It could be an intrinsic interest in a particular subject or a general interest in knowing facts—even with no further aim than knowledge itself, not even for name and fame. This varies from child to child, from mild curiosity to a voracious appetite.

But in later childhood and youth it is also possible (and often does happen) that the driving force changes from a love of approval and acceptance to the love of reputation, fame, success for the sake of success, glory, honor, and financial gain. All these loves are symptoms of the love of the world, which is the prevailing or ruling love of our middle natural level—the dominant love of our sensory level being, as we saw, the love of self and its pleasures.

When we know the quality of the ruling love at this middle natural level of our mind, we can understand the further statement that the scientifics we know can be used or abused. They are used when they form a basis for the rational level, the next highest level, which can open our mind to an inflow from our internal mind and make us wise. They are abused when they close up our mind against the influx from above, and so make us spiritually insane and irrational.

It is important to realize that this middle natural is the highest level of mental development possible for many in the learned world today, because they have ruled out the Word of the Lord as a reliable rule of conduct. This worldly level is what is often held up as the acme and aim of education. It is the goal of those who wish to produce people of cultivated intellect who will be useful citizens in Caesar's realm, but who ignore the kingdom of God.

Those who are learned, who have a great collection of all kinds of scientifics, are very much prone to believe the false idea that wisdom consists in knowing a great many facts. They are easily seduced by the idea that the more a person knows, the wiser he is, just by reason of the great amount of knowledge that he has gathered. So in some cases they mingle, with their love of the world, a certain haughtiness and pride from the love of self. Will Rogers exposed the emptiness of such an attitude when he said: "There is nothing so stupid as the educated man if you get him off the thing he was educated in."

It is also a common idea to think that because a person can reason shrewdly from sensory appearances and draw accurate conclusions from them, that he is therefore rational. From a natural, worldly point of view, he may indeed have earned the right to be considered sane and responsible, but in spiritual things, in the light of heaven, he is seen to be spiritually insane. For a truly rational view of life, we need the perspective of eternity that the Word of God gives us. Wisdom consists in doing the Lord's will from love of him. Whoever does this has wisdom, the wisdom of life, which is the only wisdom appropriate for human beings. Merely to know from sense experience a great number of laws about how people and things behave is a far cry from wisdom. Actually, we have to be regenerated to the celestial level before we are really wise. As Seneca once said, "Many a man might have attained wisdom had he not thought that he had attained it already."

Yet it is important to learn scientifics and develop a wide and varied understanding of the world around us. They open the natural mind so that it can be an adequate basis for spiritual life. They provide material by which spiritual truths may be illustrated and confirmed. How could we understand the correspondence or parallelism of natural things with spiri-

Diagram 6. The Levels of Our External Mind

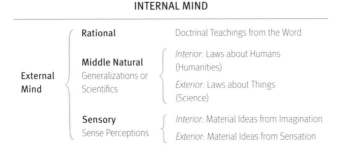

INTERNAL MIND

	Rational	Doctrinal Teachings from the Word
External Mind	**Middle Natural** Generalizations or Scientifics	*Interior:* Laws about Humans (Humanities)
		Exterior: Laws about Things (Science)
	Sensory Sense Perceptions	*Interior:* Material Ideas from Imagination
		Exterior: Material Ideas from Sensation

THE BODY

tual things if we had little or no knowledge of the laws of the natural world? How could we perform a useful function in this world without scientifics?

But to repeat: the moral virtues and decorum are the most important prerequisites for a spiritual life. Because they can later be infused with a spiritual motivation, they are an indispensable basis for spiritual life.

Diagram 6 gives a brief review of what we have seen so far. The left-hand side shows that we have discussed the natural mind as a whole, which is external to and below the internal mind. The sensory level consists of things that we experience through our physical senses—our interior and exterior sensations, the exterior sensations being simply images of material things or people that are before our senses; while our interior sensations, our imagination, consist of material ideas or images of things or people that are not yet actually present before our senses, but may be brought into reality.

All those scientifics that make up the intellect of the middle natural level, both interior and exterior, are collected together in our external or natural memory, together with the sensory images or material ideas of the sensory level below (*Secrets of Heaven* §2471). This natural memory gradually becomes quiescent after death (*Secrets of Heaven* §2476), although it can be awakened when necessary (*Secrets of Heaven* §2483). The will of the middle natural level consists of a love of the world, which manifests itself as a desire to learn about everything around us and how it works.

The exterior sensory level is limited by the quantity and richness of our sense experience, and that applies equally to the imagination, the interior sensory level, as well. The conclusions of the middle natural level are limited by the sensory level, and likewise, the rational level is limited to some extent by the middle natural level—by the quality and quantity of its scientifics. That has many implications for those who are interested in education, but this is not the place to pursue them. Now, to complete our survey of the natural mind, we must look at its highest level, the rational—the subject of our next chapter.

Our Rational Level

The term *rational* as used by Swedenborg does not mean clever reasoning, especially ratiocination (reasoning to avoid blame). It is derived from the word *ratio*, which means proportion. It is on this level of our mind that we may have a true sense of proportion. We see life in the perspective of eternity. It gives us a new view and a new set of values. The rational level, when regenerated, perceives the ratio between natural loves and spiritual loves, spiritual truths and natural truths, life in the natural world and life in the spiritual world. Whenever we evaluate our daily life in relation to our preparation for heaven, to see whether it helps or hinders it, we are using our regenerated rational level. This kind of perception is not from human nature but from the Lord alone by means of his Word.

Notice that for this to be the case, the rational level needs to be regenerated, that is, reborn from the higher levels of our mind—from the celestial or spiritual levels of our internal mind. Through the regeneration of the rational level, the heavenly loves of that internal mind flow down and into the innermost part of the rational level.

However, before regeneration, the rational level of the mind is very different. In this chapter, we will be dealing with the rational level *before* regeneration, what is often called the first or natural rational level.

The first rational level is completely natural in quality. At its worst, it has absorbed few (if any) spiritual lessons from our internal mind. The affections that make up the will side of this level are at this stage predominantly self-centered and worldly. In fact, the loves that move our first rational level and constitute its will do not belong to the rational plane of the mind at all— they belong to the sensory and the middle natural levels. (Diagram 7 shows that the will side of the first rational level is represented by a question mark.) Why? We will see why in a moment.

At best, our first rational level is characterized by dutiful, self-compelled obedience to God's commandments, unfortunately often accompanied by a feeling of having merited some kind of reward for our struggles. We have that feeling because (despite what the Word tells us) we think that we do it all ourselves, that there is no other power but our own. In this way we impose an almost unbearable responsibility on ourselves. It seems like too great a burden, so at times we are also plagued by anxiety. After all, no human being can depend on himself or herself alone all the time. Yet, because of our dutiful obedience, we are actually on the road to heaven, although we know it not.

Diagram 7. The Will and the Understanding
in Our External Mind

INTERNAL MIND

	Rational Will	**Rational Understanding**
	?	Doctrinal Teachings from the Word
External or Natural Mind	**Middle Natural Will**	**Middle Natural Understanding**
	Love of the World	Scientifics (Conclusions about the Natural World)
	Sensory Will	**Sensory Understanding**
	Love of Self	Material Ideas Based on Imagination and Sense Perceptions

THE BODY

At its worst, our natural or first rational level is hard and contentious, reveling in controversy, loving to argue from the joy of arguing, condemnatory, critical, judging unmercifully from truth alone—in short, the person is a troublemaker (*Secrets of Heaven* §1949:2).

Somewhere in between the best and the worst, our first rational level is in a state of merely natural goodness—doing good because we think it is right, not because we are moved by the Lord. Although we know and believe something from the Word of God, we still act from natural goodness. This is at the other end of the extreme from the harsh behavior described above. It is being sentimental, easygoing, and permissive. This may not seem very bad, but let us always remember that to be permissive is to permit evil, for our judgment is greatly influenced by personal bias or, on the other hand, prejudice.

As we saw above, our will on the first rational level is really from our lower levels—the middle natural and sensory levels—growing out of the love of self or the love of the world. Even the doctrinal information we gleaned from the Word of God was learned for selfish and worldly reasons, for the sake of our own aggrandizement.

Now we understand why in diagram 7 we put that question mark for the will side of our rational level. Our first or natural rational level, before it is reformed and regenerated, does not have a good spiritual love ruling it. It may have some love of the truth that is found in the Word of God, but this is used more often than not as a sword to attack others, and those others are usually considered with contempt (silently or openly) as the "weaker brethren." Hence we read that this first rational level is devoid of real goodness. It has truth, but it is separated from rational good because it is separated from higher loves from which the goodness comes (*Secrets of Heaven* §1950).

The first rational level has what could be called the "faith of authority," that is, the faith of someone else who is admired or trusted grafted into the person. It is sometimes called persuasive faith or historical faith, because it is like our faith in history. For instance, we believe that Julius Caesar was in Britain in the year 55 BCE—not because we were there at the time, nor because we have seen him, but because we believe and trust the writers of history books. Our belief in a religious system can be like that, too; believing what people have told us without testing it by living according to it. That kind of faith is merely natural in quality.

As a result, in this first or natural kind of rational level there are many obscurities, doubts, and even denials regarding the truths of faith, the true things that are to be believed. Knowing about them only from having been told about them, the merely natural rational level does not really see the truth in them or the good in them—although it thinks that it does. The underlying reason for this is that the Word of God is not really seen in its own light, the light of heaven. It is not really seen as the Lord speaking to humanity with the same power and authority as if he were physically present speaking to us. Its holiness is therefore not fully perceived.

Our attitude toward the Word of God reveals whether or not we are in the first rational stage. If, for example, we believe that the Word is only humankind's idea of God, rather than God's idea of humankind; or that the Old Testament is only the history of the Jews and the New Testament is merely the sayings of the man Jesus of Nazareth rather than the Lord's divine teaching, then we have effectively (though temporarily) destroyed in ourselves the idea of divine revelation. This is a matter of supreme importance. If the Word of God is regarded as being only a historical work produced by the varied levels of enlightenment of men of bygone ages, then our obedience to the Word of God will be only of a natural quality, and it will bring at best nothing but natural goodness and natural faith. Divine revelation should not be treated as if it were only something that keeps the theologians entertained.

Another consequence of having a natural view of the Word of God is that in this first rational level there is a great deal of pride in one's own intelligence. That is one of its most notable characteristics. A person operating on this first and natural rational level does not usually apply truth to himself, but to others, as we learn from this passage in *Secrets of Heaven*: "In the first period of our life, we know what is in the Word or what our faith teaches only by memory. We consider ourselves good when we know many things from there and can apply some of it not to our own life but the lives of others" (§3603:3).

What is commendable about this state, though, is that such a person has at least taken the trouble to learn the doctrine. Even though he has become very good at applying the truth to the life of someone else, rather than to his own life, he has thereby acquired an insight into how the truth *should* be applied. His knowledge is not entirely theoretical. This means that later, when he realizes that he ought to apply this knowledge to his own life, he will have some idea of how to do so. But in the meantime he is not yet ready to go beyond the chief characteristic of this first rational level, that is, fault finding. *True Christianity* §535 gives the reason for this. It explains that "when the truth is only in the intellect and not yet in the will, it is a common thing for people to find fault with others, and this because finding fault with others touches only the intellect, whereas finding fault with oneself is much more difficult because it touches the will."

As a result of all this, the first rational level can be critical, harsh, contentious, and unbending. This is brought out in a definitive passage in *Secrets of Heaven*:

People whose rational minds are such that they devote themselves exclusively to truth—even religious truth—and not at the same time to neighborly kindness are exactly like this. Such a person is a peevish, intolerant, universally belligerent man. He sees all others as wrong-headed, leaps to blame and criticize and punish them, lacks pity, and refuses to bother learning how to bend their minds to his way of thinking. This is because he views everything in terms of truth and never in terms of goodness. (§1949:2)

The cause of these characteristics is brought out in an adjacent passage, which points out the necessity of looking to a life of uses, that is, of useful services to others and the common good:

If we do not acquire knowledge for the sake of a useful life, the knowledge lacks any importance, because it lacks usefulness. Secular and religious knowledge by itself, without a life of service, creates the kind of rationality depicted: asslike, critical, and belligerent. This rationality has life, but it is the parched and arid life imparted by a dubious pleasure in truth tainted with conceit. (§1964:1, 2)

That is the state that the Lord was addressing when, in the Sermon on the Mount, he said, "Judge not, that you be not judged. For with what judgment you judge, you will be judged; and with the measure you use, it will be measured back to you. And why do you look at the speck in your brother's eye, but do not consider the plank in your own eye?" (Matt. 7:1–3)

It should come as no surprise to learn that the first or natural rational level loves to argue—and above all to win arguments. It even uses the truths of the Word of God as ammunition with which to shoot down in flames those who disagree. The first rational level is also characterized as being very self-righteous, or "holier than thou," because it ascribes to itself any good that it does. A person in this state speaks the Lord's truth, the truth of his holy Word, as if it were his own idea, as if he had composed it all himself. If people think that what he says is a marvelous, wonderful truth, he will agree as if it is all his own invention. And because he ascribes to himself everything good that he does, he is inclined to compare himself very favorably with other people and to be contemptuous of them in comparison with himself.

This reminds us of the Lord's parable of the Pharisee's prayer in the Gospel of Luke:

Two men went up to the temple to pray, one a Pharisee and the other a tax collector. The Pharisee stood and prayed thus with himself, "God, I thank you that I am not like other men—extortioners, unjust, adulterers, or even as this tax collector. I fast twice a week; I give tithes of all that I possess." And the tax collector, standing afar off, would not so much as raise his eyes to heaven, but beat his breast, saying, "God, be merciful to me a sinner!" I tell you, this man went down to his house justified rather than the other; for everyone who exalts himself will be humbled, and he who humbles himself will be exalted. (Luke 18:10–14)

As a further example, I recall a very telling cartoon set in a monastery, where a novice monk is saying to his superior, "But Brother Juniper, I AM holier than thou!"

Unfortunately, churches are often judged entirely by this state. People resign from churches or quietly give them up because of seeing these qualities in church members. It is unavoidable that in any given congregation there will always be some members going through this state or in the midst of it.

But it is sometimes rather difficult to decide whether the members of the church are actually in a merely natural rational state, or whether those making the criticism are in it themselves!

We would like to emphasize very strongly that while this state may be characteristic of many adolescents, it is not limited to the adolescent ages; we might stay in this first or natural rational level for our entire life on earth. We stay in it as long as we seek intellectual or spiritual truth without a regenerated will. For instance, one young Swedenborgian man, on being questioned about his continuing absence from church activities, explained succinctly, "I didn't want to be an adolescent at sixty!"

It may be of interest to know that the characteristics of the first rational level are depicted in the internal spiritual meaning of the Genesis story about Abram, Sarai, and Hagar. In the story, Sarai, Abram's wife, is unable to conceive a child. She chooses her slave-girl, Hagar, to be her surrogate. But as soon as Hagar conceives, she begins to look at Sarai with contempt, and, angered, Sarai treats her harshly. Hagar runs away to escape her mistress, but an angel comes to Hagar in the desert and orders her to return, promising that if she does so she will have a multitude of descendants. Hagar does return, and bears Abram a son, Ishmael.

As Swedenborg interprets the story, Hagar represents the love of knowing things found at the merely natural level, and Ishmael portrays the act of reasoning from that love. In the story, Ishmael is described as "a wild man" (Gen. 16:12), who most fittingly portrays this first or merely natural kind of rational level. Concerning this we read in *Secrets of Heaven*:

From the first rational [level] a person believes that he thinks truth and does good from himself, and thus from what is his own. This first rational cannot apprehend otherwise, even if it has been instructed that all the good of love and the truth of faith are from the Lord. . . .

The first rational in the beginning knows no other love than that of self and the world, and although it hears that heavenly love is altogether of another character, it nevertheless does not comprehend it. But then, when the person does any good, he perceives no other delight in it than that he may seem to himself to deserve the favor of another, or that he may hear himself called a Christian, or that he may obtain from it the joy of eternal life. (§2657:5, 6)

Whereas Hagar and Ishmael represent aspects of the middle natural level, Sarai stands for the truths of the Word, which must be allowed to reign supreme. So when the angel orders Hagar to return and submit to Sarai, what this story is teaching us is that we must submit to the truths found in the Word—the genuine spiritual teachings from the Lord—no matter how distasteful that may seem to our unregenerated middle natural or rational minds.

This story illustrates another feature of the first rational level (and another one of its great drawbacks)—that the truth has penetrated no further than into our understanding; it has not touched our will. When the truth or reality touches our will, we are smitten and humbled. We realize that the truth applies to us, and that we are basically devoid of rational good—that predominantly natural loves are driving us. We begin to understand that our will, what truly drives us, has come from beneath, whereas it should be from above.

This is what is signified in the spiritual sense of the Word of God by Ishmael, "a wild man," the illegitimate son of Abram and Hagar. This natural rational level is indeed an illegitimate rational level (*True Christianity* §451). Yet it is the only way by which we can become spiritual. It is a stage through which we must all pass. Without it, there could be no communication between the internal spiritual mind and the external natural mind: "It [the rational level] communicates with the internal man [or mind], where there is good itself and truth itself; and it also communicates with the external man [or mind], where there are evil and falsity. . . . In a word, the interior or middle man is the rational man himself, who is spiritual or celestial when he looks upward, but animal when he looks downward" (*Secrets of Heaven* §1702:2, 3).

How wonderful it would be if we were born directly into our internal mind. Love for the Lord and charity toward the neighbor would be flowing into us abundantly without any effort on our part! Yes, that is too good to be true. We actually have to enter that innermost part of our rational mind indirectly—by means of the outmost part of it. As our knowledge of the Word of God grows, we can come first into the outmost part of our rational level, which is unregenerated. This means that we have to be in a state of self-compelled obedience to the Lord's commandments. That obedience is the first step, and it forms the outmost part of our rational level. Obedience is also a characteristic of the lowest, outmost, or natural heaven, and dutifully following the commandments connects us to that level of heaven.

There is not much joy in this state; there is just self-compulsion, whether we like it or not. We are acting from duty, not from delight—a rather servile good, but nonetheless quite indispensable. We need to be very clear about the fact that our rational level can only be formed by means of instruction from the Word of God. There is no other way. It cannot be formed as the lower two levels of the mind can, simply by means of experience.

But when people hear that the rational level is formed by doctrine drawn from the Word of God, they immediately say, "How can that only relate to our natural level? Surely anything coming from the Word would make a person spiritual."

Yet that is not so; that is another important thing to understand. The mere knowledge of the truths of the Word of God does not make a person spiritual. True, no one can become spiritual without some knowledge of the truths of the Word of God, but the mere fact of knowing them does not make anyone spiritual in quality. Those truths are not spiritual in a person's mind unless they are enlightened from above, from the internal mind. When the light of heaven flows into us, we can really begin to understand what spiritual truth is, and that spiritual light flows in only to the extent that the person is shunning his evils as sins, because then good from the Lord flows in to take the place of those evils.

For example, without some enlightenment flowing in from the internal mind, the natural rational level cannot understand, in any real sense, that heavenly love is vastly different from worldly love. This is because it has not yet consciously experienced heavenly love. And yet, that love can not really be known except from the experience of at least trying to live according to what the Word of God teaches.

We have seen that the rational level in the beginning looks downward, and only by reformation and regeneration looks upward, and becomes spiritual or celestial in quality. In general, it begins by having a natural view of spiritual things. That is full of obscurities, because after all it is the will that imparts the quality, and if the will is of a natural quality, defiled by love of self and love of the world, then its view even of spiritual things can only be of a natural kind. This natural view of the Word is necessary, however, because it forms the bridge between our interior and exterior minds.

Since we all have to pass through the state of the natural rational level, we will now see how we can pass through it most quickly. The steps we need to take to achieve that desired goal will be the subject of our next chapter, in which we look at the regenerated rational level.

Our Rational Level Regenerated

Three things are needed for the regeneration of our first or natural rational level.

1. An affirmative attitude with regard to the Word of God.
2. Learning to use the truth for the sake of shunning evils (one's *own* evils) as sins against the Lord.
3. Learning to acknowledge the Lord as the only source of goodness and truth.

We are not born with these heavenly qualities. They do not belong to us, but to the Lord. He has placed them in our internal mind, that is, in the internal mind of every human being. Our task is to prepare our natural mind so that it may receive spiritual impulses from our internal mind. This we do so far as we follow the steps above, starting with changing our faulty attitude toward the Word of God.

Understanding the Word of God

The first requirement in regenerating our rational level is that the Old Testament and the New Testament need to be seen and acknowledged as the Word of God. Lifelong readers of Swedenborg's writings already do that, as do believers from many other Christian denominations and even from other religious paths. Some Swedenborgians also consider Swedenborg's writings to be revelations from the Lord, and thus equally his Word. They think of the Lord as speaking to them in those works.

This first step in the process of regeneration is therefore a complete submission to what the Lord has revealed. We cannot reason our way into the spiritual rational level, or approach it from beneath, that is, from sense perceptions and conclusions based on them. Spiritual things come from above, not from below, and so we must look upward, to the Word of God.

Probably most Christians would agree with the above statement, but Swedenborg adds a deeper dimension to our understanding of what the Word of God is: He describes the inner spiritual meaning of the Bible, what could be called its internal sense. "The Word's internal meaning . . . is the spirit that gives life to the letter; it can therefore bear witness to the Divinity and Holiness of the Word, and convince even a natural person, if he is willing to be convinced" (*Sacred Scripture* §4).

A compelling example of this internal or spiritual meaning can be seen in the Creation story in Genesis chapters one and two, as revealed verse by verse in Swedenborg's *Secrets of Heaven*. As Swedenborg describes it, the seven days of creation mean the seven stages in the regeneration of our natural mind. (This is more fully described in appendix 1.)

If we open ourselves to revelation and acquire from the Lord an unshakeable belief in his Word, we can then confirm this belief rationally and from our own experience. First, however, we must acquire that faith from above. There is a very succinct and at the same time comprehensive statement about this in *Secrets of Heaven*:

It is one thing to look at teachings on faith from the viewpoint of rational things, and something completely different to look at rational things from the viewpoint of teachings on faith. To look at teachings on faith from the viewpoint of rational things is to refuse to believe in the Word or the doctrine that comes from it until reason convinces us of its truth. To look at rational things from the viewpoint of teachings on faith, on the other hand, is to believe in the Word first, or in the doctrine that comes from it, and then use reason to confirm what it says. The first way is backward and keeps us from believing anything, but the second way is the right way and increases our belief. (§2568:2)

We are taught in that passage and in various other places in *Secrets of Heaven* that we must trust in the teachings of the Word above all else, and not allow the thought processes of our natural rational level to cause us to question those teachings. That would be to approach the Word from beneath rather than above.

One of several examples given by Swedenborg when he discusses the importance of not allowing our unregenerated rational mind to overrule spiritual teachings is the truth we discussed at the beginning of this book that all life flows in from the Lord. If the natural rational level is consulted about this, it rejects the idea, because it says, "Of course I'm a living being! I don't feel any life flowing in from the Lord. I feel as if I have life in myself. I don't need God to continue living."

If we put our faith in our own reasoning, the doubt that arises can become an outright rejection of the teaching, and once the truth is rejected, the person squanders his chance of advancing to an enlightened, spiritual rational level. When we put our faith in the Word and its teachings, spiritual light flows into us from our internal mind and begins the process of regeneration.

We have been speaking of this process in terms of individual advancement, but the same is true for a church, in the sense of a body of people working toward becoming more spiritual beings. A church also can pass through these stages of regeneration—or be stuck on one of the lower levels if the members of that church are unwilling to accept spiritual truth.

Shunning Our Evils as Sins

The second requirement for regeneration of our rational level is to shun our own evil feelings and actions as sins against the Lord. A key aspect of this step is that we must reject the evil in our nature for the Lord's sake, and for no lesser reason. Even a criminal can stop himself from committing harmful acts if he sees a policeman coming. People who operate on a purely natural level may even adopt the moral code of their community and live according to it, but they do so because they don't want to harm their reputation or risk being thrown out of the community, not because they are truly moral.

It is religion that shows us how to shun evil feelings or motives as being sins against the Lord. "How can Satan cast out Satan?" (Mark 3:23). The proper concern of religion is therefore to cleanse the inside of the cup and plate—our secret thoughts and feelings—so that as a consequence the outside—our words and actions—will be clean also (Matt. 23:26). Evil feelings such as hatred, revenge, and rejection of people of good character are to be shunned for the sole reason that they are against the Lord. So we should flee away from our evils as *sins*, which is the meaning of the verb "to shun." In the original Latin, the word usually translated as "to shun" can also mean "to flee away from." If we are going to flee away from anything at all (such as a nauseous smell), we have first of all to turn our back on it. That applies especially to our evils, including our evil feelings. As we turn our back and flee away from them, good feelings from the Lord flow in.

This brings the Lord into our life. It is a law of the spiritual world and thus of the human mind that *thought brings presence* (*Heaven and Hell* §194). Merely thinking of the Lord as a matter of faith may indeed cause him to be present in our intellect. Yet that does not make him present in our will, and thus in our life. There is love and a regard for the Lord in rejecting one's evils as sins against him. "He who has my commandments and keeps them, it is he who loves me" (John 14:21).

Looking to the Lord is a positive thing. Let no one convince you that shunning evils as sins is a merely negative matter. It involves looking to the Lord from love for him and concern for his kingdom. Can anything be more positive than that? It imparts a new spiritual quality to our life, to our motives for what we do or not do.

The next step follows automatically: doing good things because we receive those impulses from the Lord, not because we are motivated by self-interest. Concern for the Lord makes the difference between the empty good works of an unregenerated person and the truly good actions of a spiritual person. We are distinctly taught that "if we intend and do good deeds before we turn our back on evil ones as sins, our good deeds are not good" (*Life* §24); they have the quality of natural good, done for the sake of one's self and the world and not for the Lord. They only seem to be good.

We have to reject our evils and perform good actions as if of ourselves, as if we did it all by our own willpower. But afterward we need to acknowledge the truth—the reality—that if our motive was good, it was because the motivation came from the Lord. (If you would like to pursue that line of thought, read Swedenborg's short work *Life* from beginning to end.)

The genuine or spiritual kind of rational level is *formed* by truth and doctrine from the Word. There is no other way of forming it. But it is *opened* only by living a life according to those truths (*Secrets of Heaven* §5126:3). The rational level is then opened at the top to our internal mind above, and our internal mind contains nothing but good affections and true thoughts (*Secrets of Heaven* §978). These can then flow down into the rational level and regenerate it.

Acknowledging the Lord

The third requirement for regenerating our rational level is to acknowledge the Lord; that is, we have to acknowledge from the heart that any goodness and truth that we have ever had in our mind is from the Lord alone. The more we do this, the easier it becomes.

The rational level is the door to the internal spiritual mind. In his theological writings, Swedenborg sometimes describes the rational level as if it were part of the external mind, and in other passages it is treated as part of the internal mind. In the first case, the subject is the unregenerated rational level, and in the second, it refers to the regenerated rational.

In Revelation 3:20, we read: "Listen! I am standing at the door, knocking; if you hear my voice and open the door, I will come in to you and eat with you, and you with me." The rational level is the door where the Lord is standing. If we hear his voice and obey his Word (even if it is only from a sense of duty at first), we will be opening the door to let him come in and be conjoined with us.

When we say that we must acknowledge the Lord, we also need to have in mind that we mean the Lord resurrected and glorified. He is not just Jesus of Nazareth hanging on the cross, or a name, or a mere abstraction, but the Lord God Jesus Christ as a person, the Divine Person, God visible to the eyes of our mind. Without this understanding, our rational level will remain merely natural in quality.

We need to make our acknowledgment of the Lord in particular instances, each time we do something good or are tempt-ed to take credit for something we've done, not just in a general way. The more often we acknowledge the Lord in this way, the greater will be our general acknowledgment of him. In *Secrets of Heaven* we read about the importance of this: "[Without this acknowledgment] we otherwise take credit for our deeds as a matter of merit and eventually of righteousness. To claim truth and goodness from the Lord as our own is to be self-righteous. Many evils bubble up from this spring, because we then focus on ourselves in each thing we do for our neighbor, and when we do that, we love ourselves more than all others, whom we despise at heart if not with our lips" (§5758:2).

To do this is to claim for ourselves what is plainly not ours. It is spiritual thievery.

Characteristics of the Regenerated Rational Mind

From what has been presented so far, we can understand why Swedenborg spends so much time discussing the natural ra-tional state of mind and about how it can be exchanged for a spiritual one. Human nature in itself cannot be changed; it will always be selfish and worldly. But it can and must be ex-changed for what is spiritual. The transition from the natural rational mind to the spiritual rational mind is in fact a pivotal stage—nothing less than the very beginning of our reforma-tion and regeneration (*True Christianity* §571) in the innermost part of our rational level. This is where the part of us that is genuinely human begins.

The three requirements discussed above for opening—that

Diagram 8. Our Regenerated Rational Level

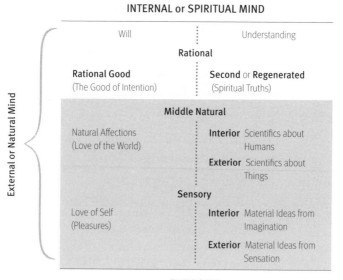

INTERNAL or SPIRITUAL MIND

	Will		Understanding
		Rational	
	Rational Good (The Good of Intention)		**Second** or **Regenerated** (Spiritual Truths)
	Middle Natural		
	Natural Affections (Love of the World)		**Interior** Scientifics about Humans
			Exterior Scientifics about Things
	Sensory		
	Love of Self (Pleasures)		**Interior** Material Ideas from Imagination
			Exterior Material Ideas from Sensation

External or Natural Mind (bracket spanning left side)

THE BODY

is, reforming and regenerating—the natural rational level really make one. We cannot really acknowledge the Lord unless we shun our evils as sins against him, and we cannot do that unless we have an affirmative attitude to his Word, where he and the heavenly life are described by divine revelation. Each of these steps is interrelated and interdependent.

We come now to diagram 8, which describes the structure of our mind as we've covered it so far. In addition to the levels building up from the bottom—the sensory level closest to our physical body, then the middle natural and the rational levels—we next see the progress of regeneration moving downward. Spiritual love and understanding are flowing down from the internal mind (where they always begin) into our second or regenerated rational level. The remainder of the chart, the gray area from the middle natural level downward, shows what is still in its natural state.

The diagram also shows that the regenerated rational level now has something on the will side, genuine rational good, which was not there before. But what is the good belonging to this rational level of our mind? How should we think of it?

It could well be called the *good of intention*, meaning that our goals truly reflect good spiritual motives from above rather than the selfish impulses of our natural rational level. When charitable motives have flowed down from our internal mind into our regenerated or spiritual rational level, that is when we begin to be in the good of intention; we seriously intend to be led by the Lord. We make a rock-firm resolution to do what he says, because he says it.

This is united with a spiritually enlightened view of the teachings that we have learned from the Word, what we have been calling spiritual truths in this book. The love that moves us has become spiritual, because spiritual teachings have been used in our life. "For everyone practicing evil hates the light and does not come to the light, lest his deeds should be exposed. But he who does the truth comes to the light, that his deeds may be clearly seen, that they have been done in God" (John 3:20, 21).

When any truth of the Word is used in our life, it is transferred from our merely *exterior* memory (where it can easily be
forgotten) into our interior memory, which belongs to the regenerated rational level of our mind. This is our "book of life"
(*Revelation Unveiled* §867). As a result of this change, we think
from that truth, not just *about* it. No longer is it merely an interesting piece of information; it has become the standard from
which we make judgments—not only about others, but also
especially about ourselves.

That goodness of the regenerated rational level is represented in the internal spiritual sense of the Word by the biblical story of Isaac, who is the *genuine* son of Abraham and Sarah.

You remember that their names had been changed from
Abram and Sarai to Abraham and Sarah by the addition of the
letter h, which is an aspirate letter, one that we breathe. That
represents the breathing in or inspiration of what is spiritual
from above. In the New Testament there is another reference
to breathing, when the Lord breathed on the disciples as he
gave them the Holy Spirit (John 20:22). His breath going forth
upon them is a perfect symbol for the divine influence flowing
forth quietly from the one and only Divine Being. That is why
the Holy Spirit is never described in the Word as a person.

Abraham and Sarah (then Abram and Sarai), you recall, had
been unable to conceive a child, and Abraham took Sarah's
handmaid, Hagar, as a mistress. Hagar conceived a son, Ishmael. Later, however, the Lord told Abraham that Sarah would
conceive, and that their son would be his heir. That son was
Isaac. After Isaac was born, Sarah told Abraham to send Ish-

mael and Hagar away—in the inner sense of the story, divine perception (Sarah) from the divine good (Abraham) orders the casting out of our first rational understanding (Ishmael) for a regenerated understanding and truly good impulses from above (Isaac).

Rebecca, the wife of Isaac, portrays this new, spiritually enlightened view of the teachings of the Word. Abraham sent a servant out to find a wife for Isaac among his own people—that is, among people who had the same faith in the Lord that Abraham did. The servant found Rebecca by a well, and knew her to be the woman he was looking for because she drew water not only for him but also for his camels. Water represents truth, and Rebecca's action means that a truly spiritual love wishes to be guided by truth, by the Word, in everyday life. Rebecca, then, stands for the enlightened spiritual truth that goes with a good intention (the will side of the regenerated mind), and is indeed married to it, showing the way. Isaac and Rebecca's life together tells us a great deal about the regenerated rational level and its relevance to life.

What are the characteristics of the rational level now that it has been regenerated?

They are the very opposite of the characteristics of the first or natural rational level. Gone from our secret thoughts and feelings is the old arrogance and contempt for others in comparison with oneself; instead there is humility in place of pride in one's own intelligence, gentleness in place of harshness, wishing well to others in place of self-centeredness, feelings of pity instead of indifference toward those suffering any affliction. The person is more patient and merciful. He or she also *rejoices* in being of use to society.

This huge change cannot be accomplished all at once, but little by little. "And the Lord your God will drive out those nations before you little by little; you will be unable to destroy them at once, lest the beasts of the field become too numerous for you" (Deut. 7:22).

As we will see in chapter 7, the heavenly qualities that have now begun to appear in the regenerated rational level have to be brought down even further, into the middle natural level and finally to the sensory level, the first part of our mind to develop while we grow but the last to be brought into heavenly order.

There are very obvious implications for our own individual regeneration in these teachings about the spiritual rational level. In other words, there are things we have to do about it. But there are also very obvious applications for any church as an organization. An ideal church has a spiritual kind of rational level—what is meant by "a rational religion." A regenerated rational level is meant to be the starting line, and a genuinely charitable life of service to others and the common good is the finishing line, the end product of a church's activities.

Every church organization on this earth has to pass through that first or Ishmael rational state. It needs to enter into it and pass through it as soon as possible, according to the Lord's order. Obviously, the more church members there are who are only at the first rational level, the more strife and personality conflicts there will be in the organization. On the other hand, the more members there are who have received from the Lord a spiritual rational level, the more peace, unity, and joy there will be in the organization.

What effects do the good affections and true thoughts belonging to the regenerated rational level have upon the levels of our mind below it as they descend into them? We will begin to explore that subject in the next chapter.

Our Middle Natural Level Regenerated

In this chapter, we will be considering the regeneration of the middle natural level of our mind. This cannot begin before the regeneration of the rational level has been largely accomplished. When that is done, the spiritual quality of our internal mind, with its genuine love and charity, begins to flow down by way of the regenerated or spiritual rational level and exercise its salutary influence upon the natural level below it.

In the previous chapter, we saw that the regenerated rational level causes us to intend what is good, that is, to intend to love the good in our neighbor and bear goodwill toward him or her. That quality is contained in our will or feeling side. On the understanding side, the function of the regenerated rational mind is to give us a certain enlightenment about how to apply to our life the principles that we have learned from the Word.

But note: the good we have received from our regenerated

rational level is only a good intention. We want to do what is good, but in the lower levels of our natural conscious mind there are still many evil impulses and mistaken ideas that hinder or even prevent us from acting out our good intentions. In order to regenerate our middle natural level, we need to take our new understanding of goodness and continue putting it into action. This is a vitally important step. We must not remain stuck with good intentions that we never apply to our lives.

In the biblical stories that represent this process, we now arrive at the stage of Isaac's old age (Genesis 27). Sensing his imminent death, Isaac knew he must bless his offspring and transfer the role of patriarch and ruler to one of his sons—to the new generation. First, Isaac summoned his eldest son, Esau, in order to bless him. In the spiritual meaning of the Word, Esau represents the will side of the middle natural level, that is, good will toward others (*Secrets of Heaven* §3305). Isaac's blessing therefore is a symbol of our own determination to live according to our spiritual understanding—to move into that state of being truly charitable.

However, this transfer from intention to life cannot be made immediately; there are many obstacles in the way. Before we can do the actual works of charity that are really good, we need to have a genuinely charitable attitude of mind, that is, a real love of others, a concern for their welfare—not only their happiness in this life, but also their eternal welfare. This love cannot be given immediately, no matter how intensely we may wish that it could.

In the literal story, the reason that Isaac could not bless Esau is that Isaac's "eyes were so dim that he could not see" (Gen. 27:1). The spiritual meaning of this is that we cannot always see how to do what we intend to do. At this stage in the process of regeneration, we are fully convinced that we should love the Lord and the neighbor; that is what we long to do. But we are in the dark about how to do it in this and that situation. There are still many attitudes lurking in the merely natural level of our mind that are contrary to loving the Lord and the neighbor.

For example: in our unregenerate middle natural level we may have learned many techniques for winning friends and influencing people. We may have found these techniques very useful for gaining a good reputation as a likeable person, and thus enhancing our worldly status. We may not have been aware that we were using them only for our own advantage. We rarely (if ever) gave a thought to our motives. We just did what came naturally. It was all so easy.

This reliance on worldly attitudes is the obstacle that prevents us from being immediately able to put our newfound spiritual insight into practice. Of course, we must have some love of the world, or we would be hermits. But we have an inordinate love of the world when we love the world and what it offers above all else. Such a love blinds the rational level to the realities of life. It cannot penetrate the darkness in the middle natural level beneath it—the evils and false ideas coming from the love of self and of the world block the light from above—so our mind cannot as yet comprehend what genuine charity is.

We are greatly deceived if we think that this darkness can be removed all at once—even as Isaac was blind and was deceived. It takes time and work.

In biblical terms, Isaac (who represents our good intentions) could not confer a blessing on Esau (a spontaneous love or concern for the neighbor). It is according to divine order that at this stage the blessing must be given to the intellect, the understanding side of the middle natural level, represented by Jacob, the other son of Isaac and Rebecca. The intellect on this natural level has to be instructed; it has to learn *how* to be really charitable in a great variety of human situations. And what is more, there needs to be a life of obedience to these new practical insights. Only then can the middle natural level be enlightened by the spiritual rational level above it.

You may recall that the intellect on the middle natural level consists of what Swedenborg calls scientifics—generalizations, both exterior and interior. The exterior laws concern the way physical objects in this world work, and interior laws concern the way human beings behave. All of these general conclusions, all these fields of learning, have to be illuminated from above by the light of spiritual rational truth so that their relevance to eternity as well as to this life is more or less clearly seen. At this stage, we may even have glimpses of understanding of divine providence.

Swedenborg helps us have this kind of perspective. He often appeals to worldly knowledge or experience to confirm the inner truths we receive from the spiritual rational level of our mind. For example, in *Divine Love and Wisdom* we read:

Those who believe in a Divine operation in all the details of nature, are able by very many things they see in nature to confirm themselves in favor of the Divine, as fully as others confirm themselves in favor of nature, in fact, more fully. For those who confirm themselves in favor of the Divine give attention to the wonders that are displayed in the production both of plants and animals. In the production of plants, how out of a little seed cast into the ground there goes forth a root, and by means of the root a stem, and branches, leaves, flowers, and fruits in succession, even to new seeds; just as if the seed knew the order of succession, or the process by which it is to renew itself. (§351)

Swedenborg then asks some penetrating questions, such as:

Can any reasonable person think that the sun, which is mere fire, has this knowledge, or that it is able to empower its heat and light to bring about these results, or is able to fashion these wonderful things in plants, and to contemplate purpose? Any man of elevated reason who sees and weighs these things, cannot think otherwise than that they come from Him who has infinite reason, that is, from God. Those who acknowledge the Divine also see and think this, but those who do not acknowledge the Divine do not see or think this because they do not wish to.

How, then, does the understanding side of our middle natural level—the part represented by Jacob—cast out the darkness that prevents our middle natural level from receiving spiritual light? This is the process represented by Jacob's years of labor for his uncle, Laban, and it is why Jacob is represented very differently before and after that time.

In the literal biblical story, Rebecca instructs Jacob to pretend to be Esau so that Isaac will be fooled into giving Jacob the blessing. Esau is furious, and plots to kill Jacob to get his blessing back. So, at Rebecca's behest, Isaac sends Jacob to La-ban to find a wife. Jacob works for Laban for many years in exchange for the promise of marrying Laban's daughter, Rachel. Jacob's years of labor represent our dutiful obedience to the truth—whether we like it or not—and our resulting victories in our battles with temptation on this natural level.

Obedience is an essential part of these "labors." Without such obedience nothing further develops. This can best be understood if we consider something else that falls into the category of knowledge represented by Jacob—moral conclusions arrived at from experience. When these are enlightened from above by the light of truth from the regenerated rational level, they take on a new quality; they are no longer merely matters of knowledge that others may have told us, but they have been transformed into true principles of life that we see inwardly for ourselves. It is as if we own them. The truth in them is seen and also the eternal good that they serve.

For instance, the virtue of courtesy may have been acquired before regeneration for the sake of social acceptance, from the merely worldly love of making a good impression. Now, however, when seen in a spiritual light, the virtue of courtesy is seen to be a means of expressing charity or love of the neighbor. We realize that we can hardly claim to love the neighbor if we are discourteous to people. Consequently, we realize the great importance of practicing courtesy in our daily life. But now we have a spiritual motivation for doing so; we realize that discourtesy is an obstacle to the Lord's coming into our mind and supping with us—that is, being conjoined with us.

However, we do have to shun discourtesy in this way many, many times before it becomes a spiritual-moral virtue and is firmly established in our minds as something truly good.

The same principle can be applied to what we know about all the moral virtues. As we live according to them from a spiritual motivation, we acquire the goodness that stems from obedience to the truth on the middle natural level. Swedenborg calls that regenerate state the "spiritual natural." It functions on the middle natural level of our mind, but the quality of its motive is now spiritual.

The valuable possessions that Jacob acquired by means of his years of labor for Laban represent spiritually the good affections gradually gained by means of sheer obedience to the truth. In the end, this is finally conjoined with a real *delight* in doing the Lord's will in our daily life, which delight is represented by Jacob's twin brother, Esau.

The joyous reunion of the two estranged brothers is very affecting to read about in the Word. This is because it describes a wondrous stage in the regeneration of our mind, namely, the joining of the goodness of obedience with a spontaneous delight in it. When this has been accomplished, the middle natural level of our mind has been fully regenerated. Swedenborg describes this happy state: "The natural [level] ought to serve the rational [level], and this the spiritual, this the celestial, and this the Lord: such is the order of subordination" (*Secrets of Heaven* §2781:9).

Diagram 9 shows what is taught in that passage a little more clearly. It shows that now the white (the goodness that

Diagram 9. Our Regenerated Middle Natural Level

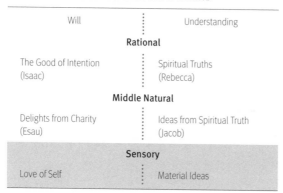

INTERNAL or SPIRITUAL MIND

Will		Understanding
	Rational	
The Good of Intention (Isaac)		Spiritual Truths (Rebecca)
	Middle Natural	
Delights from Charity (Esau)		Ideas from Spiritual Truth (Jacob)
	Sensory	
Love of Self		Material Ideas

THE BODY

flows from the internal mind) has come down one level further to the middle natural level, as well as being in the rational level. That tells us that the middle natural level should serve the rational level, and that the rational level should serve the whole of the spiritual or internal mind. Then there is a complete inflow from the inmost or highest, which is celestial love (love for the Lord). That can come down even as far as the middle natural level, since that has now been set in order.

In the previous chapter we learned that the first effect of confirming that there must be a Divine Being is at the same time the first step in the regeneration of our rational level. Now we are seeing the next result—that the middle natural level is to be reborn by what flows in from the regenerated rational level; and finally, we will see that the sensory level in us is to be brought into heavenly order as the regenerated natural level flows down into it, so that the Lord can flow in from the highest down to the lowest, or, what is the same, from the inmost to the outmost.

But at this stage the sensory level of our mind (gray in the diagram) is still closed. The sensory level is the first to be opened in a little child and the last to be controlled from above in an adult—if at all! That will therefore be the subject of our final chapter.

Our Sensory Level Regenerated

In chapter 3 we saw that our sensory level is made up of two parts: on the understanding side, there are material ideas or images that have come into our mind from things seen, heard, smelled, touched, and tasted. On the will or feeling side, we have the pleasures associated with these sensory images or experiences.

In adults, before regeneration, these pleasures are essentially selfish. In fact, the will on the sensory level is the last bastion and stronghold of the love of self, and before regeneration it consists mainly of lust for different types of sensory pleasures. When the love of self is a person's ruling or predominant love, it is the source of many evils. The understanding side of the sensory level only confirms and supports these evils, because it contains false ideas that are derived solely from the senses.

Swedenborg says that "it is difficult for the actual level of the senses, which is the lowest of the natural, to be regenerated, because it is completely filled with material ideas formed from earthly, bodily, and worldly things. Therefore, the person who is being regenerated, especially at this day, is not regenerated as to the sensory level, but as to the [middle] natural level which is next above the sensory level, to which he is raised up by the Lord from the sensory level, when he is thinking about the true things and good things of faith" (Secrets of Heaven §7442:4).

"When he is thinking about the true things and good things of faith." That is the key to being rescued from the dominion of the sensory level, for that kind of enlightened thinking brings the presence of the Lord. Without that, the person would never be able to drag himself up by his own efforts. He would be fighting against spiritual gravity!

Yet the person must fight as if he were doing it with his own willpower, all the while admitting that it is the Lord who really wages and wins the war. It is a battle between the forces of hell and heaven within the person. "In temptations, what is being fought out is whether good shall have the dominion over evil, or evil over good. The evil that wants to gain dominion is in the natural or external man, and the good is in the spiritual or internal man. If evil wins, then the natural man rules; if good wins, the spiritual man rules" (New Jerusalem §190).

No one can be fully regenerated without experiencing this inner battle and the temptations that accompany it. The reason for this is that when we experience spiritual rebirth, our old life passes away and is replaced with a new, heavenly life—we are born from above. Our sensory level experiences this as an actual death, and therefore struggles against it (*Secrets of Heaven* §8403:2).

In order to enter this fierce conflict, we have to take the initiative as if it were our own doing, examine our self, fight against the evils and false ideas of the sensory level discovered there, and shun them as sins against the Lord. This summons the Lord in his role as the Redeemer, who alone can win the battle. Swedenborg describes this in a powerful passage from *True Christianity*:

During battles or conflicts within us, the Lord carries out an individual act of redemption, much like the all-encompassing redemption he brought about while he was in the world.

While he was in the world, the Lord glorified his human [level], that is, made it divine, through battles and inner conflict. In a similar way within us individually, the Lord fights for us while we are undergoing inner conflict and conquers the hellish spirits who are assaulting us. Afterward he "glorifies" us, that is, makes us spiritual.

After this universal redemption, the Lord restructured all things in heaven and in hell in accordance with the divine design. He does much the same thing in us after crises of the spirit—that is, he restructures all the things in us that relate to heaven and the world in accordance with the divine design. (§599)

When considering the external sensory level earlier, we saw that it is like a grate or grill that sifts out what is not desired. The predominant ruling love makes the selection of what it feels ought to be fully experienced by the senses and what ought not to be attended to. If the ruling love is good and heavenly, that is, if it is motivated by love of the Lord and charity toward the neighbor, then only what is good and useful will be looked at, listened to, smelled, touched, or tasted.

This needs to be applied also to that mental activity we call imagination, which belongs to the interior of the sensory level (Secrets of Heaven §3020). As the Lord on earth said: "You have heard it was said to those of old, 'You shall not commit adultery.' But I say to you that whoever looks at a woman with lust for her has already committed adultery with her in his heart" (Matt. 5:27–28). Our imagination can be a powerful force in ourselves for good or for evil, and it is there that our dominant love is often revealed. If we fantasize about getting revenge on someone who has wronged us, or having the power to control other people's lives, or having sex with many different partners, and if we do not reject those thoughts as wrong, then they become part of us. We embrace the evils they represent, and those are the very evils that must be cast out before we can be spiritually reborn. What a different quality there would be in our mind if the mental images we admit or entertain in our imagination were always controlled by the regenerated higher levels!

In many places throughout his writings Swedenborg describes the state both of people who are subject to a regenerated rational level and those who are not, but the following passage from Secrets of Heaven may be taken as representative:

You can easily tell whether your senses come first or last, if you pay attention. If you affirm everything your senses urge or crave, and dismiss everything your intellect dictates, your senses come first. You are motivated by your appetites and are totally sense-oriented. People like this are not far from the lot of irrational animals, whose motivations are exactly the same. In fact the lot of such people is even worse than that of animals if they misuse their intellectual ability, or their rational mind, to justify the evil and falsity that their senses urge and long for. However, if you do not affirm these things but see with your inner eye that they are detours into falsity and goads to evil; if you work to chasten them and reduce them to obedience, or in other words to bring them under the control of your inner self's understanding and will; then you are reducing your senses to order by putting them in last place. (§5125:2)

Having told us what it is to have sensory things in their proper order, the same passage goes on to describe the blissful state that is the result of achieving order on the sensory level, so that the Lord reigns in a person from the first down to the last.

When our senses come last, happiness and bliss from our inner self permeate our sensory pleasures and make them a thousand times better than they were before. Sense-oriented people do not understand or believe this, are not aware of any other kind of pleasure, and do not think a higher kind exists. As a consequence, they regard the happiness and bliss within sensory pleasures as worthless. When we are ignorant of something, we do not believe it exists.

The "happiness and bliss" just described is what many people aim at as an end in itself. In this they are sadly deluded, because there is nothing more elusive than happiness when it is pursued as one's supreme goal. Whatever may be the means people use to achieve this feeling—drugs, alcohol, or the intoxication of power—they will never be successful; they will never summon that "happiness and bliss." It comes only as an unsolicited byproduct of looking to the Lord and shunning our evils as sins against him, and for no lesser reason (see *Life* §70–73). "But seek first the kingdom of God and his righteousness, and all these things shall be added to you" (Matt. 6:33).

We are completely regenerated only when celestial love flows in from our internal mind by way of the regenerated rational level and the regenerated middle natural level and replaces the love of self as the ruling or predominant love. When this happens, the understanding side of the sensory level becomes so enlightened that it sees the Lord in everything in creation. This is what is meant by the celestial level of the mind being opened; there is then an inflow from that highest level down to the lowest, to the sensory level, which is now in order. When the Lord is seen in everything around us, Swedenborg calls this "sensory truth" (*Secrets of Heaven* §1434:2).

In diagram 10, then, we see that the whole of the natural mind is white, showing that the process of regeneration has gone as far as it can go. Striving to reach that state is the purpose of life.

To the extent that we achieve that wonderful state, faith and charity are no longer mere theological terms. They are alive in our mind, so that we actually feel them! We can lift up the eyes of our thought to these higher things (or, better still, these inward things) that are not from us, but from the Lord in us, and proclaim his presence. We are free to use those deeper qualities or reject them.

A person whose sensory level has been set in order has a heavenly sense of sight, so that he abhors all forms of pornog-

Diagram 10. Our Regenerated Sensory Level

INTERNAL or SPIRITUAL MIND

Will	Understanding
Rational	
The Good of Intention	Spiritual Truths
Middle Natural	
Delights from Charity	Ideas from Spiritual Truth
Sensory	
Celestial Love (From regenerated levels above)	Sees the Lord in Everything

THE BODY

raphy; he has a heavenly sense of hearing, so that he finds blasphemy and what is called "bad language" totally abhorrent; he is disgusted by the alluring perfumes dedicated to adultery; he shuns all illicit use of the sense of touch; he turns away in disgust from the crudity of gluttony. In a word, he enjoys all five senses in the way intended by our Creator. He is completely born again.

· · · · ·

The purpose of this book has been to show in general the various levels or grades of mental activity that take place in our mind, so that we may have a distinct idea of them, and no longer think of our mind as being an amorphous mass.

It is possible to think of these levels distinctly and separately, but in actual life there is a great deal of overlap. For example, babies and infants are predominantly on the sensory level, but they may begin to use their middle natural level whenever they make generalizations about how things work and how people behave—even though at first these generalizations are made subconsciously, not explicitly. This is far from what predominates in their minds, however. They are still sensuous.

The same is true with regard to older children who are entering the adolescent stage; their minds are predominantly natural. They may occasionally think for themselves on the rational level, but this does not make them spiritually rational in the sense that Swedenborg uses that term.

Adults may have the spiritual level of their mind open, in the sense that what is spiritual flows in and has some influence on their rational level. Yet they may still be basically natural. It is the ruling or dominant love that decides which grade or qualitative level of their mind predominates. This is what decides what kind of person we are.

We need to refer these teachings to our own mind and examine our own thoughts, feelings, and motives before we can put any of this information to use in spiritual development. Diagrams or charts may well be useful to give us a fundamental idea of the subject, but we do not have a realistic view of our mind until we realize, for example, that regardless of our present character, there are also higher levels to our mind that are hidden from our everyday consciousness. Deep within ourselves we have something heavenly from the Lord. That is our potential. There are no exceptions to that.

Swedenborg's Mind

by Reuben P. Bell

The nature of the human mind is a fundamental philosophical problem that never goes away. Emanuel Swedenborg's (1688–1772) model of the mind reflects his response to the time in which he lived and worked—the early days of the Enlightenment, when the prevailing Platonic dualism was being challenged by an emerging materialism that denied the existence of anything beyond the physical world of the senses. Preserving a defensible spiritual-natural worldview while working within the limits of the new scientific method was his greatest challenge, a task that would require a methodical sifting of the entire Western philosophical tradition. To understand Swedenborg's ideas on the human mind, therefore, we must start with Plato (424–348 BCE).

Plato's system was not elaborate. There are two substances, physical and mental, with no material connection between the two. The mind was the soul, and the soul identified with the perfect world of ideal forms. This forged a composite with the physical body, and the two operated in harmony by some method not well described. But the world above was different than the world below, and their mutual interaction comprised a clear dualism of body and mind. The intellectual strength of Platonic mind-body dualism, which is perhaps best described in his *Phaedo*, was its simplicity. There is an intuitive affection for such a world that promises more than what is seen. It was for other, later philosophers to make attempts at defining the elusive nature of the interaction of body and mind.

British mathematician and philosopher Alfred North Whitehead (1861–1947) once aptly observed, "The safest general characterization of the European philosophical tradition is that it consists of a series of footnotes to Plato."[1] To this we might add that, at least in the arena of theological philosophy, people have tended to either embrace Plato's dualism in an almost intuitive way or forcefully deny it. History records little common ground between these attitudes of mutual exclusion. Once Plato's mind-body template was laid down (and this, no doubt, was derived at least in part from Pythagoras and other pre-Socratics), denial of it began to oscillate through the ages. Aristotle's immediate rebuttal led the way for others who saw no transcendence when they looked at the world or considered the operation of the mind.

Although a student of Plato, Aristotle (384–322 BCE) did not follow his master in all things. Raphael's famous painting of the pair pacing through the Lycaeum shows Aristotle's urgency for seeing things as they appear, while Plato points patiently upward, toward the source of all things.[2] Their disagreement, as depicted by Raphael, is amicable; but there is an ideological dichotomy at work here that will grow more divisive with time.

Aristotle was a master at observation and classification. His world was essentially self-contained. Plato's ideal forms have now descended to earth as products generated by physical things themselves. The soul is a function of an organized body, no longer independent or separate in any way. For Aristotle, matter and form—

mind and body—are linked in a one-dimensional composite that requires no other world, and forms do not outlive this one. Form is a product of the quality of matter to which it inheres. Plato's dualism is no longer necessary in Aristotle's hylomorphic³ world of experience, and human minds, though predictably complex, are not receivers of absolute truth. For Aristotle, the brain is an organ for cooling the blood, and the mind is little more than an appendage of the body. But, like his teacher, he offers little in the way of explanation for the marvelous things that minds can do.

With the loss of classical texts to the West, medieval scholars did not extend the thinking of the Greeks. The early Christian church had little use for pagan philosophy as a whole, and speculation on the operation of the mind—much less its operation in the body—was not much entertained. Church theologians turned their attention to matters of salvation in the Gospels and Epistles, and deep philosophy was not the order of the day. Even the Christian mystics, who would later enrich their tradition with the depth of Plato and Plotinus, were not yet looking in that direction; the simple asceticism of the Desert Fathers was setting the course of their evolution. Scholars who stand out in this period were those few who did not fit this pattern, and who blended their Christianity with first Platonic and later Aristotelian philosophy as these texts reappeared in the West.

To Augustine (354–430 CE), a complex figure with Greek classical learning and Manichaean roots, the mind was more than a merely reactive faculty; it was transcendent, as it could recognize eternal truths, and it constituted a hierarchy of capacities in a trinity of 1) senses, 2) inner senses, and 3) reason. This was new. Despite his grounding in Gnostic Neoplatonism, his ecclesiastical mind recognized how these three capacities, though separate, might be of "one substance," thereby neatly satisfying the necessities of Christian doctrine.[4] It was in such things as these that Augustine excelled: strengthening Christian doctrine with the underpinnings of Greek philosophy without diminishing the one or profaning the other. Augustine was a bridge between ancient wisdom and Christian innovation. Both were strengthened by the genius of his method. With Augustine the concept of a triune, hierarchical mind was put in play for those who would follow.

Moving from the Christian dogmatism of Augustine to the more speculative style of late medieval Scholasticism, we find in Thomas Aquinas (1225–1274) another of those thinkers who could draw elements from Greek philosophy to strengthen Christian doctrine without "paganizing" his Christianity in the process. His sources were Aristotelian texts that had reappeared in the High Middle Ages, and mining their depth of detail and breadth of content, he forged a new Christian catechism that was powered by logic strong enough to support the mystical claims of Christianity. To Aquinas, the mind was the domain of the operations of the rational faculty, namely, a dualism of intellect and will. This is no Platonic dualism, however, nor does it anticipate Descartes's dualism yet to come. These mental faculties work together as one, and combine with the body to produce a composite soul-body unit compatible with Aristotle's hylomorphic model. Along with Aristotle, Aquinas saw the soul is the form of the body, but for Aquinas the soul is a nonmaterial "intellectual soul" above the mind of reason, a "first principle of life," which can receive "universals" and live on after the death of the body as a "substantial form." What we have here is a Christian theologian devoted to Aristotle's logic and taxonomical order for the strength it can bring to Christianity, but Aquinas looks to Plato for the operation of the mind. In Aquinas's philosophy, the mind has levels, is transcendent, is linked in operation to the body in some servomechanical way, and it lives independently when this link is severed. Aquinas moves the marker forward, formulating an almost modern model of the mind. But even he does not venture to speculate on a mechanism for how these things might work.

The marker advanced again in 1620, when Francis Bacon's *Novum Organum Scientiarum* produced just what its title promised: a "new instrument of science" that would transcend the syllogistic logic of Aristotle and replace it with a new, logical method for finding truth in nature. The modern scientific method can be traced back to this date, and Enlightenment science soon became the order of the day. Old questions would now yield to more powerful methods of inquiry: a systematic ordering of experience, for proof of what had hitherto been merely speculation, but at the unfortunate expense of Aristotle's *final cause*.[5]

Rene Descartes (1596–1650), one of the first new scientists, was a mathematician and philosopher with a fascination not just for what minds do, but how. His systematic approach to the problem of where body ends and mind begins brought him very close to a new paradigm of mind. Looking back, it is easy to dismiss his errors, but considering his innovative thinking, he made major contributions to the mind/body problem. Descartes's debt to Plato is obvious: The mind is composed of spiritual *substance* that is not in space, while the body is of extended *matter*. This raises questions of an interactive mechanism that he could not readily answer, but it defined an essential operational distance between the two. The soul, or highest mind, sets humans apart from other living things. It is distinct from the body, and it may exist by itself. For Descartes, the mind is a portal for truths beyond natural apprehension, and as such it informs the body and brings order to sensory information. His is a very modern model. His efforts to explain the operation of the brain anatomically and physiologically have brought him ridicule by short-sighted modern scientists, but he was the first with the courage to try. Emanuel Swedenborg leaned heavily on this pioneer as he went about his own version of this work.

Despite the modernity of his method, Descartes relied nonetheless on *a priori* reasoning to get him past the gaps in his findings, and to move his thoughts to higher levels of operation. With Descartes we find both empirical (based on the observation) and rational (based on reasoning from self-evident propositions) methods fully at work in a combined approach for seeking truth. Reasoning from effects to causes, Descartes entered into sublime speculation on the nature of the soul. Before the new standards of *Novum Organum*, this would have been both accepted and commonplace; but now there was a tension between what could be determined from experience alone and what was seen as mere speculation. The naturalistic attitude of the Enlightenment was gaining momentum, and was soon to challenge the creative genius of the great natural philosophers yet to come.

Christian Wolff (1679–1754) followed Descartes, arguing that empirical and rational methods can and must work together to lead a scientist to the truth. In his *Psychologica Empirica* (1732) and *Psychologica Rationalis* (1734), he was the first to make the formal distinction between these two, but argued that they were one in mental operation: a base of experience guided forward by the intuitive power of reason. A popular mathematician and philosopher, he had redacted the work of Gottfried Leibniz (1646–1716) into a philosophy of his own design, and expanded the model of the mind into the abstract areas of consciousness, perception, memory, cognition, and the nature of the soul, the origin of all these qualities. He identified the two primary mental faculties as will and intellect, and speculated on the ability of the mind to know itself. His dynamic model of mind did much to bring the science of psychology into the modern era. As we shall see, it is primarily to Wolff that Emanuel Swedenborg looked in forming the framework for his own unpublished work *Rational Psychology* (1742), upon which he would build a comprehensive anatomical, philosophical, and theological model for mental activity, spiritual-natural interaction, and spiritual regeneration.

It was Immanuel Kant (1724–1804) who rejected the notion of *a priori* methodology. Inheriting preeminence among the German philosophers upon Wolff's demise, Kant made it clear in his 1781 *Critik der reinen Vernunft* (Critique of Pure Reason) that reasoning from effects to causes is not a valid pathway to the truth. In denigrating this method, he is referring to Wolff's metaphysical ideas in particular, but his anathema is pronounced on all who would employ this method in scientific inquiry. For Kant, *a priori* conclusions are paralogisms—fallacious syllogisms that rest on ambiguous terms and not on experience. Building an argument on such a flimsy foundation is bad philosophy and leads to bad science. Kant speaks with great authority, and his denial of an intuitive method lingers to this day as a caution against the use of induction in science. And yet it is the use of just this method by Swedenborg that provided the depth of his natural philosophy. A collision of ideologies emerges here, related to our second generalization concerning Plato's dualism: there are those who reject intuition out of hand.

Emanuel Swedenborg (1688–1772) came of age in the heady days of the early Enlightenment, under the influence of Bacon's "new instrument of science." From his earliest days he was dedicated to using this new method to solve the greatest problems of the natural world. But Swedenborg did not stop there. To him, these problems did not concern nature alone, but nature's interaction with the world of spiritual causes. His quest was to define both worlds, to define the interface between them, and then to explain the dynamics of spiritual-natural reality. The best place to observe these dynamics at work was in the interaction of soul and body, and he knew that to see the soul at work, one had only to look to the mind. He came equipped for the job, a student of the philosophers who had come before. He was an Aristotelian in his logic, taxonomy, and ethical forms. He was a Neoplatonist in his descriptions of layers, levels, and trines—bridging the two worlds, but in a very particular way. He found a triune mind in Augustine that could recognize eternal truths; and in Aquinas he found a rational faculty in a different kind of dualism, of intellect and will. In Descartes he found all these things and more: another dualism, of spiritual *substance* and natural *matter*, meeting at their nexus in the brain, to open the portal for spirit into nature, mind into body, to bring understanding to the mind, and order to the chaos of the senses. He would perfect this model to fit his own empirical findings of anatomy and, Kant's warning notwithstanding, to fit the rational findings of induction, too. In Wolff he found a science of mind— a *rational psychology*—that spoke of consciousness, self-knowledge, spiritual origins, and more. From the contributions of all these philosophers, he could build a model of the human mind as never before.

But Swedenborg did not stop there. To him, science becomes the first of "two foundations of truth, with the spiritual resting on the natural."[6] Taking all that had gone before, he adds footnotes of his own to Plato—his concepts of influx (the way that life, rationality, and form flow into nature from God, in a continuous creation), degrees and series (the levels of order and structure for the created universe, including both the physical and the spiritual worlds), forms (defining the spatial interaction of spirit and matter in intermediate steps, from Creator to creation), and correspondence (the causal relationship between material objects and their spiritual counterparts). With these new tools, developed by the necessity along the way, he built a functional model of the human mind that is "set up on the earth, the top of it reaching to heaven, and . . . the angels of God . . . ascending and descending upon it."[7] His model is astonishing in its completeness and its plausibility. It *works*, explaining as it does both what we see and what we know to be true about what we see. It is the bridge between the two worlds, in the order of Descartes and the complexity of Wolff, conceived from empirical observation but, Kant's warning notwithstanding, guided by the *a priori* intuition of the rational mind as well.

Such is the model of the human mind—from his collaboration with all those philosophers over all that time—that Swedenborg has given to the learned world. But there is more. The model goes beyond science, although today's science could profit greatly from the model's ability to predict and explain the psychology of our experience. It is given for the purpose of our salvation. Once understood, this working model provides a visual image of the mechanism of our spiritual regeneration: proceeding from what Swedenborg terms the rational mind at the top, through the middle natural level, to the sensory level "set up on the earth" that provides the foundation for mental life in this world—so simple, and yet so infinitely complex. *Nunc licet.*[8]

Notes

1. Alfred North Whitehead, *Process and Reality* (New York: Free Press, 1979), 39.

2. The work in question, *School of Athens*, is a fresco housed in the Vatican, originally painted in 1510–11 for Pope Julius II.

3. *Hylomorphic* is a compounding of *hyle* (matter) and *morphos* (form) to denote a single mind-body unit in which the mind is produced as a necessity of the form of the matter to which it inheres. The hylomorphic framework implies a mind that is not transcendent, that does not outlive the body, and that does not operate above or outside the body. In modern terms we might say that it is just the "brain

at work," and it is an ideology that has led from skepticism to the doctrine of scientific materialism.

4. Augustine's clearest enumeration of these ideas is to be found in his *Summa Theologiae.*

5. Aristotle's *final cause,* after the material, formal and efficient causes, was the purpose of a thing, its intangible end point or ultimate state. Bacon abandoned the teleological nature of material things when he devised a system based on sense evidence alone that necessarily excluded the immeasurable quality of a greater, transcendent design. His "new instrument of science" was by definition limited to the world of experience. Enlightenment scientists quickly expanded this concept to mean that the only truth was that which could be recognized by the senses. Thus did Bacon inadvertently plant the seed for the scientific materialism that flourishes in the modern era.

6. See Swedenborg's posthumously published work *Spiritual Experiences,* §5709, for Swedenborg's explanation of the cause-effect relationship between science and theology.

7. *Genesis* 28:12. Here in the story of Jacob's ladder is a mystical analogy for the human mind at work.

8. *True Christianity* §508:3, "Now it is allowed." Swedenborg reported seeing this proclamation over the door of a temple in the spiritual world, and he explains that it means that we are now allowed to use our intellect to explore the mysteries of faith. The saying has become a kind of motto for his contribution to the revival of the Perennial Philosophy.

Appendix 1

The Seven Days of Creation

In the literal account of the days of creation there are some obvious intellectual difficulties. For instance, there is light on the first day and the separation of day and night, and vegetation on the third day, but no sun or moon until the fourth day!

It is easy to accept that "in the beginning God created the heavens and the earth" (Gen. 1:1). How could the heavens and the earth create themselves? But it is equally clear that in the literal sense the details of how this was done contain such obvious impossibilities that no intellectually honest person can accept them as literally true and reasonable. Our discussion of regeneration in the preceding chapters can now shed a new light on the details of this familiar story.

While Swedenborg constantly affirms in page after page that the Lord is creator of the universe, he points out that "since the Word is the Lord's and comes from him, it could not possibly exist unless it held within it the kinds of things that have to do with heaven, the church, and faith. Otherwise it could not be called the Lord's Word, nor could it be said to contain any life" (*Secrets of Heaven* §2).

Accordingly, he then goes on to demonstrate verse by verse that the Creation story is not about cosmic creation but about the seven stages in the process of regeneration—the spiritual creation of an angelic kind of person. This is the kind of creation meant in the Psalmist's prayer: "Create in me a clean heart, O God, and renew a steadfast spirit within me" (Ps. 51:10).

Before this process begins, a human being is completely in the dark about spiritual things. The earth of his natural mind is a great void, and empty, devoid of spiritual thoughts and affections. "The earth was without form, and void; and darkness was on the face of the deep" (Gen. 1:2)—covered the lusts and false ideas of the unregenerate person. However, God in his mercy is working to stir up whatever remains of our childhood innocence. From this come the first rays of spiritual light. It dawns on us that there must be a God, so that we distinguish between light and darkness. This is day one.

In this new state (the "morning" of Gen. 1:5) we can make this distinction more often and more clearly. We begin to realize that our thoughts come from two different sources. Some come from our worldly mind, but others come from our newly discovered heavenly or internal mind, which is in the light of heaven. "Thus God made the firmament, and divided the waters which were under the firmament from the waters which were above the firmament; and it was so. And God called the firmament heaven" (Gen. 1:7–8). This is day two.

On the third day, the insights from the internal heavenly mind are thought about much more often. We recollect them more often. This is what is meant by the "waters under the heavens" being "gathered together [collected] into one place" in Genesis 1:9. This causes the "dry land" of our natural mind to appear—because we have earnestly examined ourselves. The spiritual aridness of our natural mind is exposed. By this we are somewhat humbled, and we begin our first works of repentance, the amendment of our lives.

These are the good works being done at this stage. They are com-
paratively inanimate, being only of the immobile vegetable kingdom in the scale of spiritual creations. The reason is that we do
not really believe yet that any good we do is from the Lord. We only
believe this because we are taught by others that this is so. Our human nature is still in everything we say and do. It is the earth—our
natural mind—that brings forth "grass, the herb that yields seed,
and the fruit tree that yields fruit according to its kind" (Gen. 1:11).
Thus day three is complete.

No further progress can be made until we acknowledge the
Lord, that he is the source, the only cause, the Father of everything
good and true. As we make this acknowledgement, our humility
increases. A new love begins to rule our mind, represented by two
great lights that appear in the *heavens*—the light of love (the sun)
and its offspring, the light of faith (the moon), coming down from
the heavenly or internal mind. When there is some love, some delight, in doing the Lord's will, then there is also something of real
faith, genuine belief; just as the light of the moon is but a reflection of the light of the sun. When this warm sunlight of the internal mind begins to shine upon the earth of our natural mind, then
for the first time the person is *spiritually* alive. This explains why the
creation of the sun and moon is so long delayed. So ends day four.

In the fifth stage of the Lord's creation of a clean heart inside
us, we really begin to make a habit of thinking from the true things
that are to be believed. They are now continually in the deepest
level of our thought as our standard of judgment, the principles by
which we evaluate, set in order, and govern everything that comes
into our mind. Note that the Lord is in these true things that are a
part of faith. He causes us to recall them and think from them. They
are his creations, in general and in each particular instance. This
is what is meant by "every living thing that moves, with which the

waters abounded, according to their kind, and every winged bird according to its kind" (Gen. 1:21). Here we see the first animate, living, spiritual states of mind. This is day five.

In the sixth stage, our chief delight and ruling love is in fostering and enhancing the good received from the Lord by the various forms of the neighbor—an individual, a group of individuals, a church, a country as a whole, the human race. These are the ascending levels of the neighbor, and helping them is love going out to others, or charity. The good in them is what we love, and that good, strictly speaking, is the neighbor. (This is why Swedenborg always says "the" neighbor rather than "one's" neighbor.) This goodwill toward others is what is meant by the "living creature" created by God on the sixth day—the animals of the earth (Gen. 1:24–25). The creation of human beings is the final dominion of the spiritual kind of love of the neighbor. We are the image and likeness of God's love and wisdom. This is the lesson of day six.

These are the six days of the Lord's labor in regeneration of a human being. It is purely the Lord's work, although it requires our cooperation, and it may appear to us as if we are doing it all ourselves.

But there is still another state: the seventh day, the sabbath of our Lord, his day of rest.

This is the state in which the person's mind is ruled, not merely by love of the neighbor, but by love going up to the Lord, the noblest and most exalted love that a human being can aim at and attain. It is the fulfillment of the first and greatest commandment, as revealed in Matthew 22:37: "You shall love the Lord your God with all your heart, with all your soul, and with all your mind."

During the first six stages, the Lord has to fight for us in our battles of temptation. But when our ruling or predominant love has become love for the Lord, the fight is over, and the holy day of rest from temptations is at hand. The Lord can then rest. This is day seven.

The Structure of Our Mind

THE SOUL

Internal Mind or Spiritual Mind	**Celestial** Love for the Lord	
	Spiritual Love toward the Neighbor (Charity)	

External Mind or Natural Mind	**Rational**	Doctrinal Teachings from the Word
	Middle Natural	*Interior:* Laws about Humans (Humanities)
		Exterior: Laws about Things (Science)
	Sensory	*Interior:* Material Ideas from Imagination
		Exterior: Material Ideas from Sensation

THE BODY

Index

Index

generalization (function), 19, 21, 37
glorification, 85
good deeds, 65, 103
good intentions, 69, 75
goodwill. See charity.

Hagar (biblical figure), 55–57, 70–71
heaven, 6, 57
heavenly level (mind). See celestial
    level (mind).
hell, 3, 6
highest (term), 17
The Human Mind, xii

images, sensory, 21
imagination, 5, 21, 32–33, 41, 86
individuality, sense of, 2
infants, 20–21, 27, 30, 35, 90
inmost (term), 17
intellect, 21, 26. See also
    understanding.
intelligence, pride in, 51–52
interior sensory level, 32–33
internal mind, 10–11, 12, 13, 15, 23,
    41, 65, 102. See also spiritual
    level (mind), celestial level
    (mind)
internal sense (of the Bible), 61–62
Isaac (biblical figure), 70–71, 75–76,
    78–79
Ishmael (biblical figure), 55–57,
    70–71

Jacob (biblical figure), 77–80
Jacob's ladder, 24–25, 99

Kant, Immanuel, 97, 98
knowledge, love of, 42, 43–44

Laban (biblical figure), 78–80
labor, spiritual meaning of, 79, 104
Leibniz, Gottfried, 96–97

life
    from the Lord, 2–3
    spiritual meaning of, 3–4
logical positivism, 15
Lord, the, acknowledging, 60, 65–66,
    68, 103
love
    biblical meaning of, 9–10
    celestial, 13, 81, 88
    heavenly vs. earthly, 58–59
    for the Lord, 10, 13, 23, 64–65,
        81, 104
    of self, 25, 35, 44, 76, 83
    of the world, 43–44, 46, 76
    See also affections, ruling love.

Marriage Love, 41
material ideas, 28, 30, 41
memory-knowledges, 37–38. See also
    scientifics.
memory, 32
    external, 21, 35, 46
    external vs. internal, 70
    middle natural level, 19, 21–22, 37–46
    external versus internal, 39–41
    regenerated, 74–82
    unregenerated, 76
mind, described, 4–14, 31. See also
    external mind, internal mind,
    natural mind, spiritual mind.
moral virtues, 40–41, 42, 45, 80

natural mind, 7, 11, 18–25, 102–103.
    See also sensory level.
natural philosophy, 39
neighbor, defined, 104
Neoplatonism, 93, 98
New Jerusalem, quoted, 84

obedience, 12, 18, 48, 57, 79–80
Odhner, Hugo, xii

Index